GREAT HITTING PITCHERS

Records Compiled by the
Society for American Baseball Research
1979 (updated 2012)

SABR, Inc.
4455 E. Camelback Road, Ste. D-140,
Phoenix, Arizona 85018.

Paperback ISBN 978-1-933599-30-4
Ebook ISBN 978-1-933599-31-1

Cover photo:
Wes Ferrell, one of the great hitting pitchers, stood out from the others like Guy Hecker, Jack Stivetts, George Uhle, Red Ruffing, and Don Newcombe, because he combined power hitting with a good batting average. A 20-game winner in six seasons, who won 193 games in all, he was the type of hitter who could hit a double and home run and knock in four runs while pitching a no-hit, no-run game (April 29, 1931). For pitchers, he hit the most home runs in a season (9) and in a career (38). He collected 52 hits in a season and knocked in a record 32 runs. He led all hurlers in slugging percentage with a career mark of .451. A fierce competitor, Ferrell played with Cleveland from 1927-33, the Red Sox 1933-37, Washington 1937-38, the Yankees 1938-39, the Dodgers 1940, and the Boston Braves in 1941. The younger brother of Rick Ferrell, Wes died in Florida December 9, 1976 at age 68.

ORIGINAL PREFACE TO THE 1979 EDITION

The Society for American Baseball research (SABR), formed in August 1971, has published an annual Baseball Research Journal since 1972. In some years the Society also publishes an additional book. In 1976, for example, SABR issued *This Date in Baseball History*, a calendar of interesting and significant baseball games of the previous 100 years. In 1978, SABR published *Minor League Baseball Stars*, the career playing records of approximately 175 minor league greats.

This year the Society is publishing *Great Hitting Pitchers*, a detailed historical account of the outstanding game, season and career records of pitchers as batters since 1876. The editor of this publication is L. Robert Davids, 4424 Chesapeake St. NW, Washington, D.C. 20016. He has had assistance in the supply and preparation of materials for this book by Robert McConnell, Cliff Kachline, Ronald Liebman, Raymond Gonzalez, Pete Palmer, John Tattersall, Paul Greenwell, Al Kermisch, and several other members of the Society.

The book sells for $2.50 to the public. Individual copies may be obtained from the editor at the above address. He also accepts your comments and criticism about this publication.

PREFACE TO THE 2012 EDITION

Welcome to a new edition of Great Hitting Pitchers, one of SABR's earliest publishing efforts. The original book was published in 1979, over thirty years ago, and as the original preface shows, sold for two-bucks-fifty. Back in those days, the Baseball Research Journal was published once a year and the Society published the occasional book. The BRJ has been a twice-a-year publication for quite some time now, The National Pastime is also in the mix, and between SABR's own publications program and our various publishing partners, we've been averaging 3-4 books a year. Now with our SABR Digital Library taking shape, that number of titles will only continue to grow.

Many of the original contributors to Great Hitting Pitchers are no longer with us. SABR's founder and the book's original editor, Bob Davids, passed on to the Elysian Fields in the sky in 2002. But new enthusiasts for baseball history and knowledge join the Society every year. Mike Cook has been instrumental in updating this book. With the help of David Vincent, he has updated the stat tables to the present day. He has also added a new chapter including the great hitting pitchers of the current era, like Mike Hampton and Micah Owings.

We hope you enjoy this new edition of Great Hitting Pitchers and welcome suggestions for what other classic SABR titles to resurrect.

Cecilia Tan
Publications Director

TABLE OF CONTENTS

Guy Hecker with Louisville in 1888

INTRODUCTION

This study of Great Hitting Pitchers traces the many *evolutionary* changes in hitting by pitchers that have taken place up to and through the one *revolutionary* change, which was the introduction of the Designated Hitter in the American League.

Batting by pitchers in the early years of major league baseball was considered pretty much a part of team play. In the very early seasons, some teams had only one regular hurler and he was expected to perform at bat much like any other players. His place in the batting order was determined by his ability and frequently it was not in the ninth spot. Because the original clubs carried only about a dozen players, the pitcher had to be an all-around performer. This must have been true as late as July 1885 because there is a reference in Sporting Life at that time that a Chicago pitcher was released not only because he had trouble getting the batters out but because he was "a weak hitter and a slow runner."

In the 1880s when the schedule increased and an additional hurler or two became part of the team, the regular hurlers frequently played at some other position on their off days. This even applied to the great pitchers of the 19th century, such as Hoss Radbourn, Pud Galvin, Tim Keefe, Mickey Welch, and John Clarkson, even though some of them were not very good with the bat. For those who were good hitters, and there were a number who were outstanding, those hurlers played so many games at other positions that they sometimes lost their distinction as men of the mound.

The rules were amended in 1891 to allow for pinch-hitting, and, although substitute batters were not used much in those days, the spare pitchers were occasionally inserted in that capacity. This was a logical move, particularly if the hurler knew how to handle his bat, because the manager had practically no bench strength.

After the turn of the century when the schedule was stabilized at 154 games and the number of players on the roster gradually increased, it was not so necessary to call on the pitcher as a substitute fielder. The first long service hurler who did not play any other position was Eddie Plank, 1901–17.

As the years passed it became more and more infrequent for a hurler to be pressed into service as an infield or outfield sub. After World War II, there were a few isolated cases where the manager shifted the pitcher to another position for one or two outs and then back to the mound. In one rare case in 1970 with the Cleveland Indians. such a shuffle resulted in southpaw Sam McDowell being placed momentarily at second base, where he had one putout.

In the 1960s, which became known as the pitchers' decade, batting averages tailed off noticeably. Pitcher batting was near rock bottom. Relief pitchers of all types were ready to come into the game at a moment's notice; right- and left-handed pinch-hitters were on the bench ready for the signal to bat for the pitcher. In 1973 the American League instituted the designated hitter. This essentially ended batting by pitchers in the Junior Circuit. The National League has held firm and pitchers there still get their licks. However, there continues to be the threat that another batter will pinch hit for the pitcher. That is understandable when the hurler leading the league in batting hits only .247, which was the case in 1979.

With that background it is readily apparent that our treatment of hitting by pitchers is essentially a historical study. It is brought up to the present time, of course, but the glory days of good hitting pitchers like Jack Stivetts, Wes Ferrell, and Don Newcombe are not expected to return.

In regard to approach to this subject, we are using a general overview first and then focusing on some of the important game records, season records, and career records. Because of the different role played by pitchers in the 19th century, we are treating that era in a somewhat different way in a separate chapter. At the end we will have a category dealing with special records. It is necessary to point out that in developing hitting records by pitchers, we have broken out those games, particularly since 1900, where hurlers played a few games at other positions. Those figures are not included in our totals. Let us use the batting record of Babe Ruth as an example. From 1914 through 1917 he was strictly a pitcher and a pinch-hitter. We include his entire batting record. In 1918 and 1919 he played some games at first base and in the outfield and he also pinch-hit. We deleted his batting record as a non-pitcher, including his record as a pinch-hitter. Why as a pinch-hitter? Well, was he a pitcher pinch-hitting or an outfielder pinch-hitting?

In Ruth's five games as a pitcher with the Yankees, we included his batting in those five games. We went even further than that. On June 1, 1920 when he pitched four innings and played outfield five innings, we included his batting record only for those four innings when he was a pitcher. That shows, possibly in an extreme way, that we differentiate between a player's batting record while pitching and while playing some other position. On pinch-hitting, it is a little more fuzzy. If the player was a pitcher most of the time during a season, we would credit his record as a pinch-hitter in his pitcher-batter totals.

PITCHER BATTING IN THE 19TH CENTURY

The hurlers who were considered the best batters of the 19th century were Guy Hecker, Bobby Caruthers, Dave Foutz, Scott Stratton, Jack Stivetts, and Win Mercer. All played a large number of games at other positions and it was a tedious process to separate out their batting records as pitchers. Does a player hit better while pitching or playing at another position? It varies to some degree. Caruthers and Foutz hit several points less as pitchers; Mercer hit .284 as a pitcher and .286 as a non-pitcher. Stivetts his .297 in each role. Stratton hit several points better as a hurler, and Hecker hit far better as a hurler. As a result, Hecker moved to the top level of 19th century pitchers with a career batting average of .305. That is a remarkable figure considering that he did not play in the 1890s when batting averages were quite high.

Hecker broke in with Louisville when the old American Association started in 1882. He became an iron-man hurler, winning 52 games and losing 20 in 1884. In his 75 games as a pitcher that year, he collected a record 92 hits while batting .302. This established him as a good solid hitter and it was typical for him to bat second or third in the line-up. Sometimes he would lead off.

The Louisville "slugger" had a banner year at bat in 1886. He pitched in 49 games (winning 26) and played outfield or first base in 35 other games. He had enough at-bats to qualify for and win the AA batting title with a .341 mark. He beat out teammate Pete Browning by one point. This resulted from his exceptionally good hitting while hurling. He batted .376 as a pitcher and only .219 while playing at other positions. His record as a hitting pitcher was climaxed by seven consecutive pitching days from August 8 to 22, 1886, during which he collected 23 hits in 34 at-bats. In the midst of this string, on August 15, in a game against Baltimore which he won 22-5, he banged out six hits in seven at-bats. These six hits included three homers (the first player to connect three times in one game) and three singles. He also got on via an outfield error and scored seven runs, which is a record for a major league player, say nothing of a pitcher. He scored 63 runs as a pitcher in 1886, far better than any other hurler. Batting high in the lineup and ahead of Pete Browning certainly didn't hurt his chances of scoring.

The big season of 1886 resulted in Hecker playing more games at first base and in the outfield. He still pitched some and hit very well when he did. He had a five-hit game in 1888 which included three doubles. Released by Louisville in 1889, he managed a poor Pittsburgh club in the NL in 1890, and while he was 2–12 on the mound, he still batted .333 in those 14 games.

The outstanding club in the AA in the 1880s was the St. Louis Browns. Pitchers Bobby Caruthers and Dave Foutz both came up in 1884. Caruthers had a won-lost record of 40–13 in 1885 and Foutz was 41–11 in 1886. Both were recognized almost from the outset as good hitters as well as good pitchers. Pitcher Foutz collected five hits in a game on May 8, 1886 and again on April 30, 1887. Caruthers had five hits in a game on May 29, 1886, and on August 16 that year he collected two homers, a triple, and a double. This was the day after Hecker had his six hits and three homers for Louisville and many thought Caruthers was robbed of a similar honor. On what looked like his third home run, he was called out at the plate on a strongly disputed play. That ended the game, which Caruthers lost 11–9, and a near riot occurred. Earlier in the game he had been called out at first by the same umpire on what the crowd thought was a safe single. This ruined his chance of hitting for the cycle, and no pitcher has ever accomplished that feat. He did wind up with four long hits and remains one of only three hurlers to achieve that distinction.

In 1887 Foutz batted .384 as a pitcher and Caruthers .370. No wonder they were used more and more at other positions. It was not unusual for one to be on the mound and the other in the outfield or at first base. The next day the roles might be reversed.

Sometimes they would change positions in the same game. They continued as teammates with Brooklyn in the AA, 1888–89, and Brooklyn in the NL in 1890–91. Both wound up their careers as non-pitchers. The sore-armed Caruthers was exclusively an outfielder in 1893, and Foutz played both first base and the outfield from 1893 to 1896 when he was managing Brooklyn. The tall, skinny playing manager (he had a build like Kent Tekulve) died of asthma in 1898 when he was only 40.

Scott Stratton broke in as a pitcher with Louisville on April 21, 1888. He was only 18 and the hometown St. Louis opponents, led by Arlie Latham, heckled the youngster unmercifully. He withstood it pretty well but the Louisville team fell apart behind him and he lost 11–7. In his second time at bat, in the fourth inning, he hit the ball over the wall for a two-run homer. He thereby became the youngest hurler to hit a round-tripper in a regulation game. In his second game on April 24 he hit a triple and a single. He batted .294 as a hurler that season and also saw some action in the outfield. A year later, on May 27, 1889, he hit a bases loaded homer at Cincinnati. Hecker, Raymond and Browning scored ahead of him. At 19 he became the youngest hurler to hit a grand slam.

Stratton won 34 games for Louisville in 1890 and also batted .333. That was his outstanding year as a pitcher in what was overall a rather mediocre career. He had two homers and a triple in a game with Chicago in 1894 and closed out his career with that club in 1895.

Jack Stivetts was another product of the old American Association. He joined St. Louis in 1889 and spent three years with the Browns before moving to Boston in the NL in 1892. He was a big strong hurler who won 33 games in 1891 and 35 in 1892. He also was a powerful hitter and frequently batted fourth or fifth. On three different occasions as a pitcher he hit two home runs in a game.

On June 10, 1890, for example, he was going into the ninth inning trailing Toledo 8–5. He had already hit two singles and a homer but when he came up in the final inning the bases were loaded. He quickly unloaded them with a grand slam to win for St. Louis 9–8. The robust pitcher hit seven round-trippers that season, the most in a season until Wes Ferrell came along many years later. Stivetts hit a total of 35 homers in his career, but a dozen came while he was playing other positions. Reduced to 20 home runs as a pitcher and three as a pinch-hitter, he lost out to John Clarkson as the top 19th century home run hitter. Clarkson hit all 24 of his while pitching.

The Wes Ferrell of his day ended his career on a low note in 1899. He played briefly with the Cleveland Spiders before giving up. That was the team that won only 20 games while losing 134. That was too much for the player known as "Happy Jack."

George "Win" Mercer came up as a pitcher with Washington in 1894. He was almost totally a hurler at first, winning 25 games in 1896 and 20 in 1897. The pitching distance had been moved back to 60 1/2 feet in 1893 and batting averages ran higher than before. Mercer hit well, was a good baserunner, and could play different positions in the field. When not on the mound he usually played third or short or in the outfield. In 1901 he hit .353 to top all pitchers. The handsome hurler was named player-manager of the Detroit team for 1903, but in January of that year took his own life in a San Francisco hotel. He was only 28.

Mercer batted .284 in his nine years as a hurler and was probably the best batting pitcher at the turn of the century. Two others good with the stick were Cy Seymour and Jim "Nixey" Callahan. However, after a period of double duty, both became full-time players and never returned to the mound. Seymour had serious control problems as a pitcher, walking 239 batters in 1898. Fortunately he was able to make a transition to the outfield and it was in that capacity that he won the NL batting championship with the Reds in 1905. Callahan had pitched a no-hit game for the White Sox in 1902, but the next year when he became manager he decided he had enough of pitching. His last game on the mound was May 8, 1903. He collected five hits in a 13–12 loss to St. Louis in 11 innings.

Thereafter he played only in the infield and outfield.

We have already mentioned two of the great batting days for pitchers in the 19th century. They came on consecutive days in 1886 when Guy Hecker collected six hits (including three homers) and scored seven runs on August 15, and when Bob Caruthers hit two homers, a triple, and a double on August 16. Reference also should be made to three other big batting days.

On September 19, 1892, Boston, with Kid Nichols pitching, ran up a score of 14–0 on Baltimore by the sixth inning. With the bases loaded in the fifth Nichols had hit a triple. The next inning the bases were again jammed when he came to the plate. Again batting left-handed (he was a switch-hitter), he hit a home run for seven RBIs in two innings. That same inning he was hit on the pitching hand by a batted ball and, after giving up three runs, he shifted to left field where Jack Stivetts changed placed with him. Stivetts was bombed by the Orioles and Boston won 14–11 in a game called in the eighth inning.

The seven runs batted in by Nichols did not constitute a game record for a pitcher, however. On June 1, 1893, Harry Staley, another Boston hurler, beat Louisville 15-4 with an exceptional display of batting power. Actually there were players on base each time he came up. According to the Boston reporter, "his two home run drives were 'corkers' and each scored three runs. His single base hit brought in two runs and his two sacrifices were instrumental in adding two more runs to Boston's score." Although the references in different papers to the sacrifice outs in the fifth and seventh innings were a little vague, Staley is credited with nine RBIs in that game. As there is no official or unofficial count of runs batted in for Hecker's 1886 game, the nine for Staley was probably the best by a pitcher until Tony Cloninger equaled that number in 1966.

Another record unique to the 19th century was the three triples hit in one game by pitcher Jouett Meekin of the New York Giants in a contest at Cleveland on July 4, 1894. However, he had a little assistance that holiday as long balls hit into the overflow crowd that lined the outfield went for three bases.

Other special batting performances by pitchers of the 19th century, such as the lists of grand slam hitters or those who hit two round-trippers in a game, are carried with those of the more recent period in a later chapter. The pitchers of the 19th century with the best batting records are listed below in chronological order. Batting records at other positions are not included. Pinch-hitting records are included if the player was primarily a pitcher during a particular season.

Period	Pitcher	AB	R	H	2B	3B	HR	AVG
1882-90	Guy Hecker	1336	259	407	47	23	12	.305
1884-92	Bob Caruthers	1114	238	310	48	19	14	.278
1884-94	Dave Foutz	858	138	234	42	19	2	.273
1888-94	Scott Stratton	788	105	220	17	19	6	.279
1889-99	Jack Stivetts	1287	219	382	61	25	21	.297
1894-02	Win Mercer	997	145	283	21	13	6	.284

Dave Foutz   Jack Stivetts

HITTING BY PITCHERS SINCE 1900

In the first decade of the 20th century the best hitting hurlers were George Mullin, Al Orth, and Jesse Tannehill. Each played a certain amount at other positions, although Mullin, a hard-working and consistent 20-game winner for Detroit, was used sparingly. As a rookie in 1902, Mullin batted .342, which stood up as his best season mark. He again led in batting in 1904 and this time collected 45 hits, a high total for a pitcher. He was used twice as a pinch-hitter in the 1909 World Series with Pittsburgh, and again led all hurlers with a .312 average with Indianapolis in the Federal League in 1914. His career batting mark was .264.

Al Orth was called the "Curveless Wonder" because he had reasonable success as a hurler relying primarily on his fastball. Although he was a big fellow at 200 pounds he could play short as well as the outfield. Playing right field for the Senators on July 18, 1903, he collected six hits in nine trips in a doubleheader, winning the first game with an RBI single. He also batted well as a pitcher that year, connecting for seven triples. That's a season record for a pitcher since 1900. Orth had two seasons in which he led all pitchers in hitting, and had a lifetime average of .278.

Albert Orth

Jesse Tannehill

Jesse Tannehill was a much better hitter than his brother Lee, a shortstop who hit only .220 over his career. Jesse was the top hitter in the initial year of the 20th century when he batted .340 for Pittsburgh. He hit .337 in 1902 but lost out to George Mullin and Bill Phillips who both hit .342. Tannehill hit safely in the first 14 games he pitched in 1902, a remarkable record for a hurler. This included one game where he worked in relief. The string ran from April 20 through July 4 when he pitched a shutout as well as hitting in his 14th straight game. He was 21 for 52 in that stretch, hitting one double, one triple, and one homer and knocking in seven runs for the Pirates. On July 7 he failed to hit in four trips against the Phils. He was used in the outfield for 16 games later in the season but did not hit very well. Tannehill, who won 20 or more games six different seasons, finished his career in 1911 with a .261 batting mark as a pitcher.

In the early teens, Doc Crandall, John McGraw's prize relief hurler on the New York Giants, was the best hitting pitcher in the majors. However, since he didn't accumulate very many at-bats in his fireman role, he had to share the laurels with another New York player, Ray Caldwell of the Yankees, and with Claude Hendrix of the Pirates. All had relatively short careers.

Hendrix, a good long-ball hitter for that period, batted .322 in 1912 and more importantly had 17 extra-base hits. This was a record for the 20th century. Included were ten doubles and six triples. He jumped to the Federal League for 1914–15 and was the top home run hitter there with two and four. With the Cubs in 1918, he led the majors with three. As a pitcher he won 23 for the Pirates in 1912 and topped the Federal League with 29 in 1914.

Caldwell's reputation as a hitter was largely enhanced by three straight days of heroics in 1915. He was used as a pinch-hitter for the Yankees in two consecutive games against the White Sox June 10 and 11. He hit a home run in each game. The next day he took his regular turn on the mound and hit another round-tripper while beating the Browns.

Caldwell was a good baserunner and a capable fielder being

used in center field for a number of games. He also was an aggressive, competitive player. The Yankees traded him to the Red Sox in 1919 but Boston soon gave up on him because he had a sore arm. The Indians picked him up and in his debut with them on August 24, 1919, he beat the A's 2–1. This was the game where he was flattened by a lightning bolt while pitching with two out in the ninth inning. He recovered after a few minutes and got Joe Dugan to ground out to end the game just as the rains came down. Two weeks later he pitched a no-hitter over his former club, the Yankees. It was a great comeback effort and he topped it off by leading all pitchers that season with a .309 batting average.

Crandall of the Giants hit about 40 points higher than either Caldwell or Hendrix, but did not have as many at-bats. He was the nominal batting champion in the National League in 1910 when he hit .342. Of course, he was far short of the necessary at-bats to qualify under modern standards to take the title from Sherry Magee, who hit .331.

Crandall had the rare distinction of hitting two triples in a game twice, on September 10, 1910, and April 15, 1911 when he worked five innings in relief. He jumped to the Federal League in 1914 and played 63 games at second base as well as pitching for the St. Louis entry. The next year he was back on the mound full-time. He received 27 walks as a batter that season, a record for a pitcher and a credit to his batting ability. Crandall finished with a career batting mark of .284, quite high for a hurler in his era.

Doc Crandall   George Uhle

There was another hurler later in the teens who made quite an impression in a short period. This was George H. Ruth, who came up with the Red Sox well into the 1914 season. The very next year he hit ten doubles, one triple and four homers and batted .315 to lead all hurlers. He was exclusively a hurler and pinch-hitter through the 1917 season. In 1918 he played some games at first and in the outfield and after the 1919 season he was almost exclusively an outfielder. Here is a summary of his hitting record. It includes his pinch-hit record from 1914–17 when he was exclusively a hurler.

Babe Ruth's Batting Record as Pitcher

Year	G	AB	R	H	2B	3B	HR	RBI	AVG
1914	5	10	1	2	1	0	0	2	.200
1915	42	92	16	29	10	1	4	21	.315
1916	67	136	18	37	5	3	3	15	.272
1917	52	123	14	40	6	3	2	12	.325
1918	20	61	12	21	9	2	2	8	.344
1919	17	54	8	14	3	2	2	12	.259
1920	1	3	2	1	0	0	0	0	.333
1921	2	3	1	1	0	0	1	1	.333
1930	1	5	1	3	0	0	0	1	.600
1933	1	3	2	1	0	0	1	1	.333
Totals	208	490	75	149	34	11	15	73	.304

Home Runs by Ruth as Pitcher

1915: May 6, June 2, June 25, July 21
1916: June 9, June 12 (PH), June 13
1917: August 10, September 15
1918: May 4, June 2
1919: May 20 (grand slam), June 21
1921: June 13
1933: October 1

The 1920 season inaugurated the era not only of long-ball

hitting, but high batting averages as well. Suddenly, pitchers were hitting well up in the .300s. In 1921, for example, Dutch Ruether hit .351, Carl Mays .343, and Jack Scott .341. In 1923 George Uhle hit .361, but was far outdistanced by Jack Bentley of the Giants, who hit .427. In 1925, Walter Johnson topped that with a fantastic season mark of .433, which was almost twice his lifetime average up to that point. The next year, the Pittsburgh Pirates had three regular starting hurlers who batted over .300: Dolf Luque .346, Pete Donohue .313, and Red Lucas .303.

Red Lucas was the National League pitcher who compiled the best hitting marks in the 1920s and 1930s. Jack Scott compiled a career batting average of .275, but he was not considered in the same "league" with Lucas. The latter was with the Braves in 1924 as a relief hurler and not being very successful played briefly at second base in 1925. Traded to Cincinnati he gradually worked into the starting rotation in 1926. He hit over .300 that year and the following two seasons and soon became recognized also as a dependable left-handed pinch-hitter.

Lucas topped the NL in pinch hits in 1929, 1930, and 1931. In 1931 he appeared in 97 games in all 29 as a starting hurler and 68 as a pinch-hitter. He pitched mostly for second division teams until moving to Pittsburgh in 1934. In 1937 he again led in pinch hits. He should have ended his career there because his batting average slipped to .109 in 1938 and his pinch-hitting record really suffered when he failed to connect in 17 at-bats. Nevertheless, he concluded his career with a sparkling .282 bat mark as a pitcher and pinch-hitter.

In the American League in the 1920s and 1930s there were three good hurlers who excelled as batters, namely George Uhle, Wes Ferrell and Red Ruffing. Uhle did not have the pinch-hitting ability of Red Lucas or the long ball capability of Ferrell or Ruffing, but he was a very strong and dependable hitter. When he batted .361 in 1923, he collected 52 hits, all as a pitcher, for a new mark in the 20th century. He had some good games and believed in winning big. On April 28, 1921 he hit two singles and a grand slam homer and knocked in six runs in an 18–5 victory. On June 1, 1923 he hit three doubles and a single, scored four runs and knocked in another four in a 17–4 triumph. Uhle topped the AL with 11 pinch hits in 1924. He was a better batter than his catcher Luke Sewell, who had a career mark of .259. Uhle's was .288, best of the long-service pitchers. He also was a first-rate pitcher, winning 26 in 1923 and 27 in 1926. He was traded to the Tigers in 1929, leaving a spot in the Cleveland starting rotation for Wes Ferrell, who was up for his first full season.

Ferrell immediately became a steady 20-game winner, but he did not make much impression as a hitter until 1931 when he broke loose with nine homers, 30 RBIs, and a .319 batting average. The previous record for round-trippers in this century was the five hit by Art Nehf of the Giants in 1924. In 1933 and 1935 Ferrell hit seven homers each year. In the latter season he collected 52 hits and had 32 runs batted in while batting .341. It was his best year. On five different occasions in his career he hit two homers in a game.

Wes came up with a sore arm in 1933 and it was feared his pitching career might be over. He played 13 games in the outfield from September 9 to October 1, collecting 13 hits in 48 at-bats for a .271 mark, about ten points below his career record as a pitcher. He had two doubles and knocked in six runs, but had no homers in that stretch. He hit 38 homers in his career, a record for a hurler. His last one came right at the end of his major league career with the Braves in April 1941. After that he played and managed in the minors, pitching only on occasion. As a regular with Marion in the Western Carolina League in 1948, he hit .425 to lead the league. He was then 40 years old.

Red Ruffing had a remarkably long career that stretched from 1924 through World War II to 1947. He was recognized as a good hitter even in those dismal years when he was losing 20 games a season with the Boston Red Sox. In 1930 he was traded to the Yankees and for that and the next two seasons, he had the highest batting average in the majors with marks of .364 in 1930, .330 in

1931, and .306 in 1932. In eight seasons of his career as a regular hurler he batted over .300. His hitting, as that of others, tailed off in the 1940s, and his career mark ended at .269. He did hit 97 doubles. a new all-time mark for pitchers, and his 273 runs batted in was the best in the 20th century.

Ruffing was a great clutch pitcher, but some criticized him for coasting when he had those powerful Yankee teams behind him. His relatively high ERA lends some support to that contention. Still he pitched 46 shutouts in an era when AL bats were blazing. One of those shutouts was a 21–0 whitewash of the Athletics on August 13, 1939. He didn't coast at bat either, collecting four hits. Exactly seven years earlier, on August 13, 1932, he went 10 innings against Al Thomas of the Senators before winning 1–0 on his own home run. That crucial game came in the period when the Yankees ran up a streak of 308 games without being blanked. Ruffing certainly saved them that day.

There were no clear-cut batting leaders in the 1940s. There were career disruptions because of World War II and most performances were spotty. Lynwood Rowe, the former "Schoolboy" with the Detroit Tigers, continued his good hitting with the Phillies until he retired after the 1949 season. He had pretty good power and had a career batting average of .263. Fred Hutchinson, who spent his entire playing career with the Tigers, had three seasons over the .300 mark and finished his career in 1953 with essentially the same batting average as Rowe.

Jim Tobin, who broke in with the Pirates in 1937 with a batting average of .441, based on 15 hits in 34 trips, could not maintain a very high average, but did hit the long ball. In 1942 he hit six home runs to tie the NL record established by Hal Schumacher of the Giants in 1934. Four of Tobin's blows came in two consecutive games. He hit a pinch homer in a game against the Cubs on May 12. The next day while pitching against the Cubs he backed Bill Nicholson against the wall for a long out his first time up and then hit three consecutive balls out of the park for a close 6–5 victory. This was the only three-homer performance in one game other than Guy Hecker's big day in 1886. Tobin was a very busy pitcher for the Braves during the war years and he did pitch a no-hit game in 1944. But he really was no great shakes on the mound. When NL batters caught up with his knuckleball in 1945, he was passed on to Detroit in mid-season. In his debut with the Tigers on August 12, 1945 before 55,000 fans in Detroit, he pitched three innings of sharp relief against the Yankees and won 9–6 with a three-run homer in the 11th inning. That was the year he tied for the lead in homers in each league with three in the NL and two in the AL. Tobin's career batting average was only .230.

Bob Lemon of Cleveland was another long-ball hitter who supported strong pitching performances (he had seven 20-victory seasons) with some timely RBIs. A former third basemen, he hit 37 round-trippers to come within one of the career record of Wes Ferrell. He also compiled an excellent .291 average as a pinch-hitter, considerably higher than his overall average of .234. His strong combined pitching and batting performance continued the Cleveland tradition established by Uhle and Ferrell.

In the 1950s, Dodger Don Newcombe was in a class by himself. He was one of the first African-American pitchers in the majors and one of the most successful, winning 27 games for Brooklyn in 1956. As a batter he not only hit the long ball, but maintained a lifetime batting average of .271. He led three times in batting average with marks as high as .359 and .361. In 1955 he had 17 extra-base hits, including seven homers, and had a .632 slugging percentage. This topped Wes Ferrell's former record of .621 in 1931. Newcombe closed out his career with Cincinnati in 1960.

With the departure of Newcombe, hitting by pitchers dropped off drastically in the 1960s. Home runs were still hit with some regularity, particularly by Earl Wilson, who hit 35 in only 740 at-bats, and Don Drysdale, with 29 in 1169 at-bats. But their career batting averages were hardly enough to scare an opposing pitcher. Wilson wound up with a .195 mark and Drysdale with .187. Bob Gibson was somewhat better with 24 homers and a .206 average. Gary Peters probably had the best overall record in this period with

Bob Lemon   Don Newcombe

a .222 career mark and a good production of extra-base hits with 31 doubles, 7 triples, and 19 homers in only 807 at-bats. He also is the only pitcher ever to hit four pinch homers.

In the 1970s, Catfish Hunter had a good one-year performance when he hit .350 for Oakland in 1971. However, that was well above his usual capabilities. Also, the DH came along in 1973 and practically cut off his opportunities. He wound up his career at .226 and with six home runs.

The batting leader in the 1970s was Ken Brett, although the DH also reduced his appearances. Nevertheless, he was the only AL hurler to get a fair test as a hitter since the DH came in in 1973. In 1976 with the White Sox, he went to bat 12 times while pitching. Unfortunately, he collected only one single, which reduced his career average somewhat. His lifetime mark through 1979 is .262 based on 91 hits in 347 at-bats. He has hit ten homers.

Brett also was one of the last pitchers to be used as a pinch-hitter. On May 27, 1974, when he was with the Pirates, he slammed a pinch triple to knock in two runs in a win over the Padres in the second game of a twin bill. In the opener he hurled a 6–0 victory and singled in a run. Brett had the highest average of any hurler in 1974, with a .310 mark.

The older brother of George Brett gained national attention in

June 1973 when he connected for one home run in each of four consecutive starting assignments for the Phils. The dates were June 9, 14, 18 and 23. In the game prior to this streak on June 3, Brett was pitching at San Francisco and this is what took place. In the sixth inning with Boone on second, Brett hit a long drive which cleared the right-field fence. Umpire Dick Stello signaled that it bounced over the fence and held Brett up at second base. After the game, center fielder Garry Maddox of the Giants told this story.

"I turned to Bobby (RF Bobby Bonds) and asked him why Brett was standing on second. Bobby told me it was because the umpire called it a double and for me to keep my mouth shut." Manager Ozark said that nobody on the bench could see the drive clearly and, thus, nobody protested. Brett said, "I wasn't watching the ball and I didn't think it was going out so I stopped on second when the umpire told me to."

As a result, Brett had an extra-base hit in five consecutive games, but his home runs were officially limited to four games.

TOP GAME BATTING PERFORMANCES

One of the significant batting achievements for pitchers is getting five hits in one game. This has happened very seldom in baseball history. Possibly it should be mentioned right at this point that Lou Gehrig, in his 2164 games, during which he compiled a batting average of .340, never collected five hits in one game. Therefore, it shouldn't be so surprising to note that teammate Red Ruffing never had five hits in a game, and they both played in some very high scoring games. In the game that Ruffing won 21–0 over the Athletics on August 13, 1939, the opportunity was reduced when the "contest" was called after eight innings. Red wound up with four hits.

Back on June 17, 1936, Ruffing participated in a multiple massacre of the Cleveland Indians which had some unusual features for the pitchers. The Yankees won 15–4 and 12–2, collecting 19 hits in each game. Ruffing won the opener, banging out four hits, including two home runs. In the nightcap, Monte Pearson pitched a steady game while driving out four hits and driving in four runs. It was probably the only twinbill where both winning hurlers had four hits each.

Two pitchers worked consecutive games where they batted out four hits in each contest. George Earnshaw of the Athletics performed the feat June 9 and 13, 1931, getting a homer in each game. Kirby Higbie, when he was with the Dodgers, duplicated the feat August 11 and 17, 1941, getting a double in each game. Neither developed into an outstanding hitter in those two seasons, Earnshaw hitting .263, and Higbie only .188.

We have already mentioned that in 1886 Guy Hecker had a phenomenal streak where he had 23 hits in seven consecutive pitching assignments. On August 12 he was 4-for-5 and on August 15 he was 6-for-7. His six hits in a game, of course, was tops for all pitchers. He also had another game, in 1888, where he had five hits, including three doubles. It was more common for pitchers to achieve five hits in those days. Dave Foutz also did it twice. In the first place, if they were good hitters, they batted higher in the lineup. Of the first ten pitchers to collect five or more hits, one batted second, three batted third, one fourth, one sixth, one seventh, one eighth, and one ninth.

Jim "Grasshopper" Whitney of Boston, probably the best hitting pitcher in the National League in the 1880s, was batting leadoff when he banged out five hits in a tremendous 30–8 rout of Detroit on June 9, 1883. He went to bat eight times and scored six runs, which was the record until Hecker came along six years later. Unfortunately, Whitney cannot be included among the pitchers with five hits in a game because he played part of the game in center field.

When it came to getting five hits in a game as a pitcher, Jim "Nixey" Callahan stood out. He did it three times. The first was with the Chicago Colts (Cubs) on June 29, 1897. He was the hurler in that record-breaking 36–7 triumph over Louisville and contributed to the cause with five hits in seven trips. The next time was May 18, 1902 when Callahan was with the White Sox. He hooked up in a pitching duel with Red Donahue of the Browns and they battled to a 2–2 tie in 17 innings. Jim knocked in both runs for the ChiSox while going 5-for-8. On May 8, 1903, he went 5-for-6 in an 11-inning loss to the Browns. That was the last game he pitched in the majors.

Since then the five-hit game by pitchers has been achieved only seven times in 75 years. Of those, Babe Ruth probably had the best performance, collecting a triple, three doubles, and a single in a 10-inning loss for the Red Sox on May 19, 1918. One reason he lost was that he didn't knock in any runs with his five hits. He did drive out four long hits and that has been achieved only three times by pitchers. Ironically, Johnny Murphy, who seldom went to bat five times in a game because of his primary role as a relief hurler, collected five singles on August 28, 1936 and knocked in five runs.

There follows the list of pitchers with five hits in a game from 1876 through 2011.

Date	Pitcher and Club	AB	R	H	2B	3B	HR
May 14, 1884	Charles Radbourn, Prov. NL	7	4	5	0	0	0
May 22, 1885	Charles Buffington, Bos. NL	6	3	5	1	0	0
June 4, 1885	Hardie Henderson, Bal. AA	5	2	5	1	0	0
June 6, 1885	Robert Emslie, Bal. AA	6	4	5	1	1	0
May 8, 1886	Dave Foutz, StL. AA	6	2	5	1	1	0
May 13, 1886	Henry Boyle, StL. NL	6	2	5	1	0	1
May 29, 1886	Bob Caruthers, StL. AA	6	3	5	1	1	0
August 15, 1886 (2)	Guy Hecker, Lou. AA	7	7	5	0	0	3
April 30, 1887	Dave Foutz, StL. AA	7	3	5	2	1	0
June 6, 1888	Guy Hecker, Lou. AA	6	3	5	3	0	0
August 25, 1889	Phil Ehret, Lou. AA	5	1	5	0	1	0
July 16, 1890	Tom Ramsey, StL. AA	5	1	5	1	0	0
June 8, 1893	Sadie McMahon, Bal. NL	5	1	5	1	0	0
May 20, 1895	Clark Griffith, Chi. NL	5	1	5	0	0	0
August 25, 1896	Tom Breitenstein, StL. NL	5	1	5	1	0	0
June 29, 1897	Jim Callahan, Chi. NL	7	4	5	2	0	0
May 18, 1902	Jim Callahan, Chi. AL	8	0	5	0	0	0
May 8, 1903	Jim Callahan, Chi. AL	6	2	5	2	1	0
May 19, 1918	Babe Ruth, Bos. AL	5	1	5	3	1	0
May 6, 1922	Vic Aldridge, Chi. NL	5	1	5	0	0	0
May 22, 1925	Pete Donohue, Cin. NL	5	1	5	0	0	1
August 1, 1928	Henry Johnson, NY AL	5	0	5	0	0	0
August 14, 1935	Lynwood Rowe, Det. AL	5	3	5	0	1	0
August 28, 1936	Johnny Murphy, NY AL	5	3	5	0	0	0
September 26, 1964	Mel Stottlemyre, NY AL	5	1	5	1	0	0

Two or More Home Runs in a Game

Most of the great batting days by pitchers of the past revolve around home runs. Some hurlers may have had trouble keeping up their batting average, but they could on occasion stroke the long ball. Part of the explanation might be that pitchers generally have been bigger and taller than other players. Whatever the reason, hurlers have had some big home run games.

There were two pitchers who hit three home runs in a game. Some of us still remember when Big Jim Tobin did it for the Boston Braves May 13, 1942. He had to provide his own batting support to beat the Cubs 6–5. The other one was the oldtimer, Guy Hecker of Louisville, who did it against St. Louis on August 15, 1886. He had considerable help from his teammates, as well as scoring seven runs himself, and won 22–5.

Jim Tobin, who hit three home runs in a game, shown here in a Detroit uniform in 1945.

There were no fewer than 66 other occasions when hurlers hit two home runs in a game. Several hurlers did it more than once, most notable among them being Wes Ferrell, who hit dual round-trippers on five occasions. Jack Stivetts did it three times before 1900 and Don Newcombe three times since 1950. Red Ruffing, Lew Burdette, Jack Harshman, Dick Donovan, Pedro Ramos, Tony Cloninger and Rick Wise did it twice. At least two of these feats merit special mention.

Tony Cloninger hit two round-trippers in a game on June 16, 1966. Only two weeks later, on July 3, he again hit two in a game, and they were both grand slams. He also had a single and knocked in nine runs, a record for a pitcher. Rick Wise also had a couple of two-homer games in the summer of 1971, but the surprising thing about the first time, on June 23, was that he didn't neglect his pitching either. He tossed a no-hit, no-run game against the Reds.

Relief pitchers are not restricted from the two-homer sweepstakes. Dixie Howell hurled less than four innings for the White Sox on June 16, 1957, but still came through with two circuit smashes. In addition, two Tiger hurlers Jess Doyle in 1925 and Babe Birrer in 1955 both hurling the last four innings, came up twice and connected both times. For Birrer it was two three-run belts, and that was probably why they called him "Babe." Another pitcher hit two homers while in "relief," but it was in relief of an outfielder. On May 8, 1906, Chief Bender went to the A's outfield midway in the game to replace an injured player. Later coming to bat, he hit two four-baggers, a feat he was never able to accomplish while pitching.

Ironically, some of the hurlers who hit two homers in a game never connected again in their careers. One of these was Ed Summers of the Detroit Tigers on September 17, 1910. The Detroit Free Press reporter had a field day reporting this unusual event.

> "Never since the birth of our National Pastime has a more startling chapter been contributed to its history than that which Eddie Summers produced yesterday... To end the reader's suspense, the big pitcher got two home runs in the same game in successive times at bat, on each occasion scoring a man ahead of him. Krause was the opposing pitcher. He was led from the field on the verge of a mental collapse."

The writer went on at length describing Summers as "the worst hitter in the world," and how, in his first time up he fanned "in the helpless manner that has made him famous." The writer stated that both of the home runs were "aided by the ball yard's architecture" and he was right about that. On the first one, Summers swung late at the ball and sliced it over first baseman Harry Davis' head. It bounced fair and twisted into the stands back of first for an official home run. The second drive was described as a hard one down the left-field line which bounced into the stands well back of third. He also hit a single. All this hitting made it a very unusual game for Summers. He never came close to hitting another home run.

Here is the full list of pitchers hitting two or more home runs in a game. Note that two AL hurlers achieved the two-homer performance on the same day. July 31, 1935.

Three Home Runs in a Game

Date	Pitcher and Club
Aug. 15, 1886 (2)	Guy Hecker, Lou. AA
May 13, 1942	Jim Tobin, Bos. NL

Two Home Runs in a Game (see next page)

Date	Pitcher and Club	Date	Pitcher and Club
May 3, 1883	Monte Ward, N.Y. NL	July 6, 1952	Ben Wade, Bkn. NL
May 27, 1884	Fred Goldsmith, Chi. NL	April 14, 1955	Don Newcombe, Bkn. NL
October 9, 1884	John Clarkson, Chi. NL	May 30, 1955 (2)	Don Newcombe, Bkn. NL
August 16, 1886	Bob Caruthers, StL. AA	July 9, 1955	James Hearn, N.Y. NL
August 13, 1887	John Clarkson, Chi. NL	July 19, 1955	Babe Birrer, Det. AL
June 12, 1888	Bob Caruthers, Bkn. AA	September 19, 1956	Don Newcombe, Bkn. NL
June 10, 1890	Jack Stivetts, StL. AA	June 16, 1957 (2)	Dixie Howell, Chi. AL
August 6, 1891	Jack Stivetts, StL. AA	July 14, 1957 (1)	Billy Hoeft, Det. AL
June 1, 1893	Harry Staley, Bos. NL	August 13, 1957	Lew Burdette, Mil. NL
July 27, 1894	Scott Stratton, Chi. NL	July 10, 1958	Lew Burdette, Mil. NL
July 4, 1895	Frank Foreman, Cin. NL	July 16, 1958 (2)	Jack Harshman, Bal. AL
June 12, 1896	Jack Stivetts, Bos. NL	August 23, 1958	Don Drysdale, L.A. NL
April 20, 1898	Cy Young, Clev. NL	September 23, 1958	Jack Harshman, Bal. AL
September 17, 1910	Ed Summers, Det. AL	September 2, 1960	Don Cardwell, Chi. NL
June 30, 1912	Ed Willett, Det. AL	July 2, 1961	Glen Hobbie, Chi. NL
May 2, 1919	James Shaw, Wash. AL	August 27, 1961	Milt Pappas, Bal. AL
July 29, 1924	Arthur Nehf, N.Y. NL	May 18, 1962	Dick Donovan, Clev. AL
July 4, 1925 (2)	Tony Kaufmann, Chi. NL	May 30, 1962 (1)	Pedro Ramos, Clev. AL
September 10, 1925 (1)	Garland Buckeye, Clev. AL	August 31, 1962	Dick Donovan, Clev. AL
September 28, 1925 (2)	Jess Doyle, Det. AL	July 31, 1963 (2)	Pedro Ramos, Clev. AL
June 24, 1926 (1)	Jack Knight, Phil. NL	August 16, 1965	Earl Wilson, Bos. AL
July 22, 1930	Phil Collins, Phil. NL	June 16, 1966	Tony Cloninger, Atl. NL
September 18, 1930	Red Ruffing, N.Y. AL	July 3, 1966	Tony Cloninger, Atl. NL
August 31, 1931	Wes Ferrell, Clev. AL	July 7, 1969	Jim Rooker, K.C. AL
August 31, 1932	Elon Hogsett, Det. AL	June 23, 1971	Rick Wise, Phil. NL
April 24, 1934	Hal Schumacher, N.Y. NL	August 28, 1971 (2)	Rick Wise, Phil. NL
July 13, 1934	Wes Ferrell, Bos. AL	September 1, 1971	Ferguson Jenkins, Chi. NL
August 22, 1934	Wes Ferrell, Bos. AL	September 2, 1971	Sonny Siebert, Bos. AL
July 31, 1935	Wes Ferrell, Bos. AL	September 5, 1976	Larry Christenson, Phil. NL
July 31, 1935	Mel Harder, Clev. AL	September 30, 1978	Randy Lerch. Phil. NL
June 17, 1936 (1)	Red Ruffing, N.Y. AL	August 6, 1983	Walt Terrell, N.Y. NL
August 12, 1936 (1)	Wes Ferrell, Bos. AL	May 12, 1985	Jim Gott, S.F. NL
August 14, 1937 (1)	Eldon Auker. Det. AL	May 1, 1990	Derek Lilliquist, Atl. NL
June 16, 1940 (2)	Jack Wilson, Bos. AL	August 8, 2000	Darren Dreifort, L.A. NL
July 26, 1940	Spud Chandler, N.Y. AL	June 5, 2001	Mike Hampton, Col. NL
May 7, 1941	William Lee, Chi. NL	June 2, 2002	Robert Person, Phi. NL
May 20, 1945	Bucky Walters, Cin. NL	August 11, 2004	Randy Wolf, Phi. NL
July 7, 1949	Dave Koslo, N.Y. NL	September 20, 2006	Dontrelle Willis, Fla. NL
July 24, 1949	Bob Lemon. Clev. AL	August 18, 2007	Micah Owings, Ari. NL

HURLERS HITTING GRAND SLAMS

Pitchers have contributed significantly to the grand slam story, and this is not a reference to all the bases-loaded home runs served up by journeymen starters and relievers. It was a National League hurler, Bill Duggleby of the Phils, who was the first and only player ever to hit a grand slam in his first at-bat in the majors. This feat was accomplished on April 21, 1898, in a game against the New York Giants. Cy Seymour, a fastball pitcher with poor control, got one over the middle of the plate in the second inning, and Duggleby put it over the fence.

The first pinch home run with the bases loaded was hit by pitcher Mike O'Neill of the Cardinals, who went in to bat for pitcher Ed Murphy in the ninth inning on June 3, 1902. He hit one of Charlie Pittinger's pitches to the center-field wall at Boston and he chased all three baserunners home, including his brother Jack O'Neill, in a victory over the Beantowners.

It also was a pitcher who was the only NL player to hit two grand slams in one game. This was Tony Cloninger of the Atlanta Braves on July 3, 1966, which we noted earlier.

The list of pitchers who hit grand slam homers is embellished also by the names of great American League hurlers such as Walter Johnson, Babe Ruth, Lefty Grove, Wes Ferrell, Red Ruffing, and Early Wynn. Burly Early did it as a pinch-hitter, and we thought those instances should be included because calling on a hurler to pinch hit with the bases loaded is quite a compliment. In Wynn's case he hit his slam in the fifth and then pitched the rest of the way to win the game.

Seven hurlers hit two bases-loaded homers in their careers. In addition to Cloninger, there were Lynwood Rowe and Tommy Byrne, each of whom hit one as a pinch-batter, and Dizzy Trout, Camilo Pascual, Bob Gibson, and Rick Wise. Dave McNally of the

Orioles hit one in regulation play and one in the World Series. Byrne and Al Hollingsworth were the only grand slam hitters who also gave up slams to other pitchers. Lon Warneke, who never hit one himself, suffered the embarrassment of giving up two jackpot wallops to fellow pitchers.

What were the most exciting grand slams? Well, any bases-loaded homer by a pitcher is dramatic, but Ruffing hit his full-house homer in the bottom of the ninth with the score tied 2–2. Clay Bryant hit one in the tenth to win a game for the Cubs in 1937. This was the only extra-inning slam by a pitcher and was unusual because Bryant was pitching in relief of Charlie Root, who had homered earlier in the game. On May 16, 1953, Byrne, then with the White Sox, had the distinction of batting for Vern Stephens, who was then one of the active leaders in grand slams with 10. He came through with a jackpot poke in the ninth inning against Ewell Blackwell of the Yankees.

Grand Slams Hit by Pitchers in 19th Century

Date	Hurler-Hitter & Team	Opposing Hurler	Inn.
June 20, 1882	Larry Corcoran, Chi. NL	J. Richmond, Wor.	9
April 27, 1887	Bob Caruthers, StL. AA	G. Pechiney, Clev.	8
May 27, 1889	Scott Stratton, Lou. AA	Leon Viau, Cin.	7
September 4, 1889	Tom Lovett, Bkn. AA	Elmer Smith, Cin.	4
June 10, 1890	Jack Stivetts, StL. AA	Fred Smith, Tol.	9
June 27, 1891	Clark Griffith, StL. AA	John Dolan, Col.	7
July 15, 1891	George Haddock, Bos. AA	Frank Dwyer, Cin.	7
April 30, 1892	Ice Box Chamberlain, Cin. NL	Frank Foreman, Was.	8
September 19, 1892	Kid Nichols, Bos. NL	George Cobb, Bal.	6
May 28, 1894	Harry Staley, Bos. NL	Ch. Petty, Wash.	8
August 28, 1897	Chick Fraser, Lou. NL	Brickyard Kennedy, Bkn.	6
April 21, 1898	Bill Duggleby, Phil. NL	Cy Seymour, N.Y.	2
August 2, 1899	Bert Cunningham, Lou. NL	Bill Carrick, N.Y.	5

Grand Slams by National League Pitchers Since 1900

Date	Batter	Pitcher	Inn.
June 3, 1902 PH	Mike O'Neill, StL.	Pittinger, Bos.	9
May 24, 1907	Pat Flaherty, Bos.	G. Wiltse, N.Y.	2
July 22, 1910	Chas. Phillippe, Pitt.	F. Miller, Bkn.	2
September 22, 1910 (2)	Geo. Ferguson, Bos.	Rowan, Cin.	3
April 28, 1921	Lee Meadows, Phil.	J. Scott, Bos.	8
June 8, 1924	John Watson, N.Y.	Morrison, Pitt.	2
May 12, 1925	Jimmy Ring, Phil.	Aldridge, Pitt.	6
June 23, 1929 (2)	Phil Collins, Phil.	Greenfield, Bos.	2
May 5, 1930	Bill Walker, N.Y.	French, Pitt.	4
May 10, 1931	Fred Fitzsimmons, N.Y.	Malone, Chi.	2
July 17, 1934 (1)	Roy Parmalee, N.Y.	Warneke, Chi.	7
May 28, 1936	Al Hollingsworth, Cin.	Warneke, Chi.	2
August 28, 1937 (2)	Clay Bryant, Chi.	Gabler, Bos.	10
April 26, 1938	Curt Davis, StL.	Hollingsworth, Cin.	4
May 19, 1941	Claude Passeau, Chi.	Casey, Bkn.	2
May 2, 1943 PH	Lynwood Rowe, Phil.	Javery, Bos.	6
September 7, 1947	John Miller, Chi.	Higbie, Pitt.	2
July 3, 1949	Monty Kennedy, N.Y.	Martin, Bkn.	7
September 24, 1950	Erv Palica, Bkn.	Church, Phil.	5
July 10, 1958	Lew Burdette, Mil.	Podres, L.A.	4
August 1, 1959	Bob Purkey, Cin.	Buzhardt, Chi.	3
August 9, 1961	Don Drysdale, L.A.	Nottebart, Mil.	2
August 2, 1962	Art Mahaffey, Phil.	Anderson, N.Y.	3
July 15, 1963 (1)	Carl Willey, N.Y.	Johnson, Hous.	2
September 29, 1965	Bob Gibson, StL.	G. Perry, S.F.	8
July 3, 1966	Tony Cloninger, Atl.	Priddy, S.F.	1
(same game)	Tony Cloninger, Atl.	Sadecki, S.F.	4
May 20, 1967	Jack Hamilton, N.Y.	Jackson, StL.	2
July 28, 1968	Al McBean, Pitt.	Jaster, StL.	5
September 4, 1970	Mike Corkins, S.D.	Merritt, Cin.	4

Grand Slams by National League Pitchers Since 1900 (cont.)

Date	Batter	Pitcher	Inn.
August 28, 1971 (2)	Rick Wise, Phil.	McMahon, S.F.	7
September 16, 1972	Burt Hooton, Chi.	Seaver, N.Y.	3
July 26, 1973 (1)	Bob Gibson, StL.	Strohmayer, N.Y.	5
August 21, 1973	Rick Wise, StL.	Harrison, Atl.	3
June 24, 1974	Jim Lonborg, Phil.	Taylor, Mon.	3
July 6, 1977	Don Stanhouse, Mont.	Bonham, Chi.	2
September 27, 1977	Larry Christenson, Phil.	Lamp, Chi.	7
August 26, 1979	Bruce Kison, Pitt.	Shirley, S.D.	2
October 1, 1980	Enrique Romo, PIT	R.L. Jackson, NYM	8
September 11, 1982	Scott Sanderson, MON	Martz, CHC	3
May 15, 1984	Joaquin Andujar, STL	Dedmon, ATL	8
May 16, 1984	Steve Carlton, PHI	Valenzuela, LAD	4
September 12, 1985	Don Robinson, PIT	Brusstar, CHC	8
August 10, 1986	Bob Forsch, STL	Bielecki, PIT	5
May 29, 1995	Chris Hammond, FLA	Reynolds, HOU	2
June 27, 1995	Denny Neagle, PIT	Bullinger, CHC	6
August 25, 1995	Jeff Juden, PHI	Cummings, LAD	4
September 7, 1996	Donovan Osborne, STL	Ashby, SDP	5
July 20, 1998	Kevin Tapani, CHC	Neagle, ATL	3
September 2, 1998	Kent Mercker, STL	J. Sanchez, FLA	4
May 24, 2000	Shawn Estes, SFG	M. Johnson, MON	5
September 29, 2001	Denny Neagle, COL	Haynes, MIL	4
June 2, 2002	Robert Person, PHI	Chen, MON	1
July 7, 2006	Dontrelle Willis, FLA	Lima, NYM	4
September 22, 2008	Jason Marquis, CHC	Niese, NYM	4
October 1, 2009	Chris Carpenter, STL	Wells, CIN	2
May 21, 2010	Brad Penny, STL	Pineiro, LAA	3
July 4, 2011	Shaun Marcum, MIL	D. Hudson, ARI	4
August 31, 2011	Jake Westbrook, STL	Wolf, MIL	4

Grand Slams by American League Pitchers Since 1900

Date	Batter	Pitcher	Inn.
July 18, 1906	Fred Falkenberg, Wash.	Owen, Chi.	6
June 21, 1914	Walter Johnson, Wash.	Boehler, Det.	5
May 5, 1919	Jim Shaw, Wash.	Johnson, Phil.	2
May 20, 1919	Babe Ruth, Bos.	Davenport, StL.	2
April 28, 1921	George Uhle, Clev.	Leonard, Det.	4
April 14, 1933	Red Ruffing, N.Y.	Weiland, Bos.	9
July 27, 1935	Robert Grove, Bos.	Blaeholder, Phil.	2
August 12, 1936 (1)	Wes Ferrell, Bos.	Lisenbee, Phil.	4
July 21, 1937 (1)	Lynn Nelson, Phil.	Andrews, Clev.	8
June 10, 1938	Monty Stratton, Chi.	C. Wagner, Bos.	2
July 22, 1939 (2)	Lynwood Rowe, Det.	Potter, Phil.	2
July 26, 1940	Spud Chandler, N.Y.	Appleton, Chi.	9
July 15, 1945 PH	Zeb Eaton, Det.	Borowy, N.Y.	4
May 8, 1948	Carl Scheib, Phil.	Gillespie, Chi.	8
July 28, 1949	Dizzy Trout, Det.	Gettel, Wash.	9
June 23, 1950	Dizzy Trout, Det.	Byrne, N.Y.	4
July 23, 1950	Saul Rogovin, Det.	Lopat, N.Y.	2
August 6, 1950 (1)	Ellis Kinder, Bos.	Pierce, Chi.	5
September 15, 1946 PH	Early Wynn, Wash.	Gorsica, Det.	5
September 18, 1951 (1)	Tommy Byrne, StL.	Hudson, Wash.	9
May 5, 1953	Bob Porterfield, Wash.	Wight, Det.	4
May 16, 1953 PH	Tommy Byrne, Chi.	Blackwell, N.Y.	9
April 22, 1956	Don Larsen, N.Y.	Sullivan, Bos.	4
April 15, 1959	Bob Grim, K.C.	Latman, Chi.	3
August 14, 1960 (1)	Camilo Pascual, Wash.	Turley, N.Y.	6
May 30, 1962 (1)	Pedro Ramos, Clev.	Estrada, Balt.	6
May 31, 1963	Orlando Pena, K.C.	Rudolph, Wash.	5
April 27, 1965	Camilo Pascual, Minn.	Williams, Clev.	1
July 20, 1965	Mel Stottlemyre, N.Y.	Monboquette, Bos.	5
August 13, 1966	Earl Wilson, Det.	Osinski, Bos.	7
June 1, 1967	John O'Donoghue, Clev.	McLain, Det.	6
May 5, 1968 (1)	Gary Peters, Chi.	Downing, N.Y.	4
August 26, 1968 (1)	Dave McNally, Balt.	C. Dobson, Oak.	1
July 9, 1969 (1)	Fred Talbot, Seattle	E. Fisher, Cal.	6
May 11, 1971	Steve Dunning, Clev.	Segui, Oak.	2
June 23, 2008	Felix Hernandez, SEA	Santana, NYM	2

A review of the best one-game batting performances by a mounds-man since 1900 results in a list that is difficult to cut off. Various factors have to be weighed, such as hits, runs, extra bases, and RBIs. The best batting show was probably Tony Cloninger's two grand slam homers and a single for nine runs batted in. Babe Ruth (and many other great sluggers) never had nine RBIs in a game. In Ruth's greatest batting day as a pitcher, he had five hits, including three doubles and a triple, but not one RBI in ten innings. Lew Wiltse, older brother of George Wiltse of the Giants, was the only other pitcher since 1900 to have four long hits in a game. He had two doubles and two triples while pitching the A's to a 13–0 win over the Senators in 1901.

Allowing for Ruth, who played 10 innings, all the other one-game efforts listed below were for nine innings except for Vic Raschi and John Odom, who played six innings, and Babe Birrer, four. The latter, in a relief appearance, hit two three-run homers in two trips, the greatest batting effort by a fireman. The tabulation below is concerned only with the plate performance; the pitching results are given only for general interest.

Pitcher and Club	"Bat Day"	AB	R	H	2B	3B	HR	RBI	Outcome
Tony Cloninger, Braves	July 3, 1966	5	2	3	0	0	2	9	Won 17-3
James Tobin, Braves	May 13, 1942	4	3	3	0	0	3	4	Won 6-5
Lew Wiltse, Athletics	August 10, 1901	5	4	4	2	2	0	3	Won 13-0
Babe Ruth, Red Sox	May 9, 1918	5	1	5	3	1	0	0	Lost 4-3
Wes Ferrell, Red Sox	August 12, 1936	4	2	3	0	0	2	6	Won 6-4
Spud Chandler, Yanks	July 26, 1940	5	2	3	0	0	2	6	Won 10-2
Jack Harshman, Orioles	September 23, 1958	3	2	3	1	0	2	3	Won 3-2
Vic Raschi, Yanks	August 4, 1953	4	2	3	1	0	0	7	Won 15-0
George Uhle, Indians	June 1, 1923	4	4	4	3	0	0	4	Won 17-4
George Uhle, Indians	April 28, 1921	5	2	3	0	0	1	6	Won 18-5
Pete Appleton, Nats	May 30, 1937	5	1	4	0	1	0	6	Won 11-4
John Odom, Athletics	May 4, 1969	3	1	3	1	0	1	6	Won 11-7
Babe Birrer, Tigers	July 19, 1955	2	2	2	0	0	2	6	Save

Red Ruffing, who batted over .300 in eight seasons and who led all hurlers in batting average in four seasons.

BEST SEASON HITTING RECORDS

A review of the annual listing of pitchers with the highest batting average will indicate most of the top hitters of the 20th century. The only star missing seems to be Red Lucas, who nevertheless had several seasons over the .300 mark. The top batting average, based on a minimum of 70 at-bats a season, varies widely from year to year. There were some outstanding season batting averages compiled in the 1920s, while in the 1960s it was just the opposite.

It is interesting to note that Walter Johnson, who was regarded by many to be the best pitcher in baseball, also had the highest season batting average with .433 in 1925. There is no logical explanation why the Big Train had such an outstanding year at the plate, particularly so late in his career. It certainly wasn't because of good health. Johnson was out four weeks in mid-year with influenza and ailing tonsils and two weeks at the end of the season because of a pulled muscle. He made only 30 appearances as a pitcher but came through with his twelfth 20-victory season.

Johnson entered the 1925 season with a lifetime .226 batting mark. However, he had gradually improved his hitting and in 1924 had pushed his season mark up to .283.

New Orleans researcher Paul Greenwell, who analyzed Sir Walter's game-by-game record in 1925, found that Johnson's 42 hits in 97 at-bats included some real crucial blows. For example, on April 23 he hit a two-run pinch double in the ninth inning to beat Herb Pennock and the Yankees 2–1. Similarly on May 19, he defeated the Indians in the ninth inning with a pinch two-run homer 4–3. Even in a 5–0 loss to Bullet Joe Bush of the Browns on August 27, Johnson collected the only Washington hit, a sixth inning double. In consecutive victories over the A's September 1 and 7, Johnson went 3 for 4 in each game to solidify the only .400 season for a pitcher in AL history.

Johnson's game-by-game record in 1925, compiled by Paul Greenwell, is carried below.

Date	Opponent	Place	AB	H	XBH	RBI	Comments
Apr 18	Philadelphia	A	3	1	-	-	Lost 3-0
Apr 22	New York	H	4	1	-	1	Won 10-0
Apr 23	New York	H	1	1	2B	2	Pinch hit
Apr 28	Boston	A	3	1	3B	-	Won 9-2
May 6	Boston	H	3	1	-	-	Won 10-8
May 11	Chicago	A	3	2	-	2	Won 9-0
May 16	Cleveland	A	4	2	-	-	Won 6-2
May 19	Cleveland	A	1	1	HR	2	Pinch hit
May 21	Detroit	A	4	3	-	1	Won 6-2
May 23	Detroit	A	1	0	-	-	Pinch hit
May 27	Philadelphia	A	3	1	-	1	Won 10-9
May 28	Philadelphia	A	1	0	-	-	Pinch hit
May 28	Philadelphia	A	2	1	-	-	Lost 9-4
Jun 1	New York	A	3	2	-	-	Won 5-3
Jun 6	Chicago	H	3	0	-	-	Won 4-1
Jun 11	Detroit	H	2	0	-	-	Lost 7-4
Jun 16	St. Louis	H	4	2	2B	1	Won 3-0
Jun 21	Cleveland	H	3	1	-	1	Lost 7-5
Jun 26	Philadelphia	A	4	0	-	-	Won 5-3
Jun 30	Philadelphia	H	4	2	2B	1	Won 7-0
Jul 28	Chicago	H	1	1	-	-	Lost 10-5
Jul 29	Chicago	H	1	1	-	1	Won 8-6 (Rel.)
Aug 2	Detroit	H	3	2	-	-	Won 5-1
Aug 6	St. Louis	H	4	1	-	-	Won 10-3
Aug 9	Cleveland	H	3	2	-	1	No decision
Aug 13	Cleveland	H	2	2	-	-	No decision
Aug 18	Cleveland	A	4	1	-	1	Won 7-4
Aug 20	Cleveland	A	1	0	-	-	Pinch hit
Aug 22	Detroit	A	3	2	HR	3	Won 20-5
Aug 24	Detroit	A	1	0	-	-	Pinch hit
Aug 27	St. Louis	A	3	1	2B	-	Lost 5-0
Sep 1	Philadelphia	H	4	3	2B, 2B	-	Won 7-3
Sep 7	Philadelphia	A	4	3	-	-	Won 2-1
Sep 11	Boston	H	3	0	-	-	Won 5-4
Sep 17	Detroit	H	2	0	-	1	Lost 12-9
Sep 20	Chicago	H	2	1	-	1	No decision
Totals			97	42	9	20	W-20 L-7

JOHNSON'S BATTING AGAINST EACH TEAM

W-L	Team	AB	H	AVG
3-0	Boston	9	2	.222
3-1	Chicago	10	5	.500
2-1	Cleveland	18	9	.500
3-2	Detroit	16	7	.438
2-0	New York	8	4	.500
5-2	Philadelphia	25	11	.440
2-1	St. Louis	11	4	.364
20-7		97	42	.433

Jack Bentley's .427 batting average with the Giants in 1923 was easily the best in the National League. The closest in the 20th century was the .381 mark compiled by Curt Davis with the Cardinals in 1939. Other top one-season marks were the .364 by Red Ruffing in 1930, the .361 by George Uhle in 1923 and .361 by Don Newcombe in 1958.

Ruffing had the top average for four different seasons, including three in a row, 1930–32. Newcombe finished first in three. and George Mullin also led in three, including one when he was in the Federal League in 1914. Babe Ruth was one of six who won two titles. Steve Carlton was the top hitter in both 1977 and 1978.

In light of the modest batting averages of pitchers in recent years, it came as some surprise to see two regular pitchers on the Pirates' staff in 1974 with averages of over .300. They were Ken Brett with a .310 average in 87 at-bats, and Jim Rooker with a .305 average in 95 at-bats.

The annual leaders in best batting average are carried below. Selection is based on a minimum of 70 at-bats a season. The only time we have dipped below this level is when a hurler with slightly fewer than 70 at-bats had a much better batting average than his closest competitor.

Year	Pitcher and Club	H	AB	AVG
1900	Jesse Tannehill, Pitt. NL	32	94	.340
1901	Win Mercer, Wash. AL	24	68	.353
1902	George Mullin, Det. AL	38	111	.342
	Bill Phillips, Cin. NL	39	114	.342
1903	Cy Young, Bos. AL	44	137	.321
1904	George Mullin, Det. AL	45	152	.296
1905	George Wiltse, N.Y. NL	20	72	.278
1906	Jesse Tannehill, Bos. AL	22	79	.278
1907	Al Orth, N.Y. AL	33	102	.324
1908	Al Orth, N.Y. AL	20	69	.290
1909	Bill Bailey, StL. AL	21	73	.288
1910	Doc Crandall, N.Y. NL	25	73	.342
1911	Jack Coombs, Phil. AL	45	141	.319
1912	Claude Hendrix, Pitt. NL	39	121	.322
1913	Otto Hess, Bos. NL	26	83	.313
1914	George Mullin, Ind. FL	24	77	.312
1915	Babe Ruth, Bos. AL	29	92	.315
1916	Jeff Pfeffer, Bkn. NL	34	120	.283
1917	Babe Ruth, Bos. AL	40	123	.325
1918	Pete Schneider, Cin. NL	24	83	.289
1919	Ray Caldwell, Bos./Cle. AL	21	68	.309
1920	Burleigh Grimes, Bkn. NL	34	111	.306
1921	Dutch Ruether, Bkn. NL	34	97	.351
1922	Elam Vangilder, StL. AL	32	93	.344
1923	Jack Bentley, N.Y. NL	38	89	.427
1924	Wilbur Cooper, Pitt. NL	36	104	.346
1925	Walter Johnson, Wash. AL	42	97	.433
1926	Dolf Luque, Cin. NL	27	78	.346
1927	Joe Shaute, Clev. AL	27	83	.325
1928	Burleigh Grimes, Pitt. NL	42	131	.321
1929	George Uhle, Det. AL	37	108	.343
1930	Red Ruffing, Bos./N.Y. AL	40	110	.364
1931	Red Ruffing, N.Y. AL	35	106	.330
1932	Red Ruffing, N.Y. AL	38	124	.306
1933	Ed Brandt, Bos. NL	30	97	.309
1934	Lynwood Rowe, Det. AL	33	109	.303
1935	Wes Ferrell, Bos. AL	52	150	.347
1936	Bill Swift, Pitt. NL	31	105	.295
1937	Lynn Nelson, Phil. AL	30	90	.333
1938	Vern Kennedy, Det. AL	23	79	.291
1939	Curt Davis, StL. NL	40	105	.381

Year	Pitcher and Club	H	AB	AVG
1940	Vern Kennedy, StL. AL	25	84	.298
1941	Red Ruffing, N.Y. AL	27	89	.303
1942	Chubby Dean, Phil. AL	27	101	.267
1943	Lynwood Rowe, Phil. NL	36	120	.300
1944	Eddie Lopat, Chi. AL	25	81	.309
1945	Nelson Potter, StL. AL	28	92	.304
1946	Oscar Judd, Phil. NL	25	79	.316
1947	Johnny Sain, Bos. NL	37	107	.346
1948	Carl Scheib, Phil. AL	31	98	.316
1949	Harry Brecheen, StL. NL	21	77	.273
1950	Fred Hutchinson, Det. AL	31	95	.326
1951	Mel Parnell, Bos. AL	25	81	.309
1952	Gene Bearden, StL. AL	23	65	.354
1953	John Lindell, Phi./Pit. NL	31	97	.320
1954	Bob Rush, Chi. NL	23	83	.277
1955	Don Newcombe, Bkn. NL	42	117	.359
1956	Jim Wilson, Bal./Chi. AL	23	77	.299
1957	Harvey Haddix, Phil. NL	21	68	.309
1958	Don Newcombe, Cin./L.A. NL	26	72	.361
1959	Don Newcombe, Cin. NL	32	105	.305
1960	Jim Perry, Clev. AL	22	91	.242
1961	Curt Simmons, StL. NL	20	66	.303
1962	Camilo Pascual, Minn. AL	26	97	.268
1963	Gary Peters, Chi. AL	21	81	.259
1964	Tony Cloninger, Mil. NL	21	87	.241
1965	Don Drysdale, L.A. NL	39	130	.300
1966	Juan Marichal, S.F. NL	28	112	.250
1967	Luis Tiant, Clev. AL	18	71	.254
1968	Jim Maloney, Cin. NL	18	74	.243
1969	John Odom, Oak. AL	21	79	.266
1970	Bob Gibson, StL. NL	33	109	.303
1971	Jim Hunter, Oak. AL	36	103	.350
1972	Claude Osteen, L.A. NL	24	88	.273
1973	Steve Renko, Mont. NL	24	88	.273
1974	Ken Brett, Pitt. NL	27	87	.310
1975	Bob Forsch, StL. NL	24	78	.308
1976	Rich Rhoden, L.A. NL	20	65	.308
1977	Steve Carlton, Phil. NL	26	97	.268
1978	Steve Carlton, Phil. NL	25	86	.291
1979	Rick Sutcliffe, L.A. NL	21	85	.247

The list of pitchers leading in home runs hit each season indicates that the era of hard-hitting hurlers began long before Wes Ferrell came on the scene. In the 1880s and 1890s there were some substantial totals considering that the total home runs hit at that time were not large. Jack Stivetts had seven in a season, John Clarkson and Bill Hutchison six, and Jouett Meekin and Pink Hawley five each. This made up for the drought in 1880–81 when no pitcher hit a four-bagger. This was not surprising because some of the team totals were minuscule three, four, and five home runs in a season. There was another stretch from 1899 to 1913 when no hurler hit more than two in a season.

Here are the annual leaders in the major leagues since 1876.

Pitchers Leading in Home Runs Hit, 1876-2011

1876 John Manning 1
1877 Jim Devlin and Frank Larkin 1
1878 Monte Ward 1
1879 Monte Ward 2
1880 (none)
1881 (none)
1882 Jim Whitney 4; Jim McCormick and John Richmond 2
1883 Monte Ward 5; J. Whitney 4; Radbourn, Welch, and Mountain 3
1884 Guy Hecker 4; J. Clarkson, M. Welch, T. Keefe, and F. Mountain 3
1885 John Clarkson 4
1886 Guy Hecker, John Clarkson, and Bob Caruthers 3
1887 John Clarkson 6; Tony Mullane, Ed Seward, and Bill Terry 3
1888 Bob Caruthers and Pete Conway 3
1889 Ad Gumbert 5; Scott Stratton 3
1890 Jack Stivetts 7; John Luby 3
1891 Jack Stivetts and Frank Foreman 4
1892 Frank Killen 4; Kid Gleason 3
1893 Frank Killen 4; J. Stivetts, J. Meekin, and A. Rusie 3

1894 Bill Hutchison 6; J. Meekin 5; J. Stivetts 4; A. Rusie 3
1895 Pink Hawley 5; John Taylor 3
1896 Cy Young 3
1897 Kid Nichols 3
1898 Fred Klobedanz 3; Nichols, Seymour, Young, and Doheny 2
1899 (fourteen tied with one)
1900 Ted Breitenstein and Frank Hahn 2
1901 Griffith, Donovan, Nichols, Powell, and Waddell 2
1902 Christy Mathewson and Mike O'Neill 2
1903 Jack Chesbro 2
1904 F. Owen, B. Duggleby, T. Fisher, and P. Flaherty 2
1905 Cy Young and Christy Mathewson 2
1906 Bill Duggleby 2
1907 Harry Howell and Ed Karger 2
1908 Doc Crandall 2
1909 Orval Overall 2
1910 Walter Johnson, Ed Karger, and Ed Summers 2
1911 Jack Coombs, Joe Wood, and Doc Crandall 2
1912 Walter Johnson, Ed Willett, and Grover Alexander 2
1913 J. Duboc, W. Johnson, O. Hess, and H. Sallee 2
1914 Walter Johnson 3
1915 Ray Caldwell, Babe Ruth, and Claude Hendrix 4
1916 Babe Ruth and George Tyler 3
1917 Babe Ruth 2
1918 Claude Hendrix 3; Babe Ruth 2
1919 Jim Shaw 3; Babe Ruth 2
1920 Jack Quinn and Leon Cadore 2
1921 Roy Moore, Henry Meadows, and Fred Toney 3
1922 Wilbur Cooper 4
1923 Ted Blankenship 3
1924 Art Nehf 5; Jim Wingard 3
1925 Garland Buckeye, Jack Bentley, and Dizzy Vance 3
1926 Wayland Dean 3
1927 Ted Blankenship, Milt Gaston, and Jim Wingard 3
1928 Jim Elliott 3

1929 Ervin Brame 4; Earl Whitehill 3
1930 Red Ruffing and Pat Malone 4
1931 Wes Ferrell 9; Fred Fitzsimmons 4
1932 Robert Grove 4; Red Ruffing 3
1933 Wes Ferrell 7
1934 Hal Schumacher 6; Wes Ferrell 4
1935 Wes Ferrell 7; Lynwood Rowe 3
1936 Wes Ferrell and Red Ruffing 5
1937 Eldon Auker and Lynn Nelson 3
1938 Thornton Lee 4
1939 Auker, McKain, Cooper, Lohrman, Root, and Tobin 2
1940 Spud Chandler, Bob Feller, Vern Kennedy, and Jack Wilson 2
1941 Claude Passeau and Whitlow Wyatt 3
1942 Jim Tobin 6
1943 Lynwood Rowe 4; Spud Chandler and Jim Tobin 2
1944 Dizzy Trout 5
1945 Jim Tobin 5; Bucky Walters 3
1946 Dizzy Trout and Claude Passeau 3
1947 Clint Hartung 4; Dizzy Trout 3
1948 Bob Lemon 5; Gene Bearden 2
1949 Bob Lemon 7; Clint Hartung 4
1950 Bob Lemon 6; Clint Hartung 3
1951 Bob Lemon and Eddie Lopat 3
1952 Jim Hearn and Ben Wade 3
1953 Johnny Lindell 4; Larsen, Porterfield, Wynn, and Nuxhall 3
1954 Joe Nuxhall 3
1955 Don Newcombe 7; J. Antonelli, J. Hearn, and W. Spahn 4
1956 Jack Harshman 6; Bob Lemon 5
1957 Hal Jeffcoat and Maury McDermott 4
1958 Don Drysdale 7; Jack Harshman 6
1959 Don Drysdale 4; Jerry Casale and Don Newcombe 3
1960 Don Cardwell 5; Warren Spahn 3
1961 Don Drysdale 5; Warren Spahn 4
1962 Dick Donovan and Milt Pappas 4
1963 Gary Peters, Pedro Ramos, and Bob Gibson 3

1964 Earl Wilson 5; Gary Peters 4
1965 Don Drysdale 7; Earl Wilson 6; Bob Gibson 5
1966 Earl Wilson 7; Tony Cloninger 5
1967 Earl Wilson 4; Dave Giusti 3
1968 Earl Wilson 7; Dave McNally 3
1969 John Odom 5; Lew Krausse and Jim Rooker 4
1970 John Odom, Jim Merritt, and Ferguson Jenkins 3
1971 Rick Wise, Sonny Siebert, and Ferguson Jenkins 6
1972 Bob Gibson 5; Tom Seaver and Steve Dunning 3
1973 Ken Brett 4; M. Corkins, C. Morton, and R. Wise 3
1974 Roric Harrison 3; K. Brett, T. Griffin, and J. Montefusco 2
1975 Larry Christenson 2
1976 Larry Christenson and J.R. Richard 2
1977 S. Carlton, L. Christenson, R. Rhoden, and T. Seaver 3
1978 Randy Lerch 3; Dave Roberts 2
1979 J. Andujar, J. Bibby, J. Richard, and T. Seaver 2
1980 Bob Forsch 3
1981 (nine tied with one)
1982 Tim Lollar and Rick Rhoden 3
1983 Walt Terrell 3
1984 Tim Lollar, Eric Show, and Fernando Valenzuela 3
1985 Jim Gott 3
1986 Rick Aguilera, Dennis Eckersley, Bob Forsch, and Mike LaCoss 2
1987 Brian Fisher and Bob Forsch 2
1988 David Palmer 2
1989 Don Robinson 3
1990 Derek Lilliquist 2
1991 Tommy Greene 2
1992 (twelve tied with one)
1993 Dwight Gooden, Tommy Greene, Chris Hammond, and Armando Reynoso 2
1994 (seven tied with one)
1995 Steve Avery, John Smiley, and Fernando Valenzuela 2
1996 Steve Avery, Dave Burba, Jim Bullinger, Shane Reynolds, and

Jason Isringhausen 2
1997 Joey Hamilton 2
1998 Kerry Wood 2
1999 Alex Fernandez 3
2000 Darren Dreifort 3
2001 Mike Hampton 7
2002 Mike Hampton 3
2003 Brooks Kieschnick 3
2004 Randy Wolf 3
2005 Livan Hernandez, Eric Milton, and Brad Hennessey 2
2006 Carlos Zambrano 6
2007 Micah Owings 4
2008 Carlos Zambrano 4
2009 Carlos Zambrano 4
2010 Yovani Gallardo 4
2011 Zach Duke, Cliff Lee, Kevin Millwood, and Carlos
  Zambrano 2

That takes care of the best season batting averages and the leading home run hitters among hurlers. What about the other batting categories? The season leaders in hits, runs, doubles, triples, runs batted in, and slugging percentage since 1900 are listed here with only the following commentary. It is noteworthy that almost every department has a different leader. Also, it is apparent that pitchers from the 1960s and '70s made little contribution in these departments on a seasonal basis. In fact, except for Earl Wilson and Don Drysdale in home runs, as noted earlier, those hurlers have been practically shut out. For example, no hurler active in the last few years has hit seven triples in his career (though Dontrelle Willis is close, with six as of 2011), say nothing of one season, like Al Orth did in 1903.

Most Hits by a Pitcher in One Season
52 George Uhle, Cleveland AL, 1923
52 Wes Ferrell, Boston AL, 1935

49 Carl Mays, New York AL, 1921
45 George Mullin, Detroit AL, 1904
45 Jack Coombs, Philadelphia AL, 1911
44 Cy Young, Boston AL, 1903

Most Runs
31 Jack Coombs, Philadelphia AL, 1911
27 Ray Caldwell, New York AL, 1915
25 Claude Hendrix, Pittsburgh NL, 1912
25 Wes Ferrell, Boston AL, 1935
24 Wes Ferrell, Cleveland AL, 1931
23 George Uhle, Cleveland AL, 1923

Most Doubles
13 Joe Wood, Cleveland AL, 1912
13 Red Ruffing, Boston AL, 1928
12 Walter Johnson, Washington AL, 1917
12 Joe Bush, St. Louis AL, 1925
11 Red Lucas, Cincinnati NL, 1933
10 George Mullin, Detroit AL, 1904
10 Elam Vangilder, St. Louis AL, 1922
10 George Uhle, Cleveland AL, 1923
10 Bucky Walters, Philadelphia NL, 1936
10 Bill Swift, Pittsburgh NL, 1936

Most Triples
7 Al Orth, Washington AL, 1903
6 Kid Nichols, Boston NL, 1901
6 Jesse Tannehill, Boston AL, 1904
6 Claude Hendrix, Pittsburgh NL, 1912
6 Walter Johnson, Washington AL, 1913
5 Cy Young, Boston AL, 1901
5 Lew Wiltse, Balt./Phil. AL, 1902
5 Jake Thielman, St. Louis NL, 1905
5 Russell Ford, New York AL, 1910
5 Erskine Mayer, Phil./Pitt. NL, 1918

Most Runs Batted In
32 Wes Ferrell, Boston AL, 1935
30 Wes Ferrell, Cleveland AL, 1931
28 Lynwood Rowe, Detroit AL, 1935
26 Lynn Nelson, Philadelphia AL, 1937
26 Bob Lemon, Cleveland AL, 1950
25 Ervin Brame, Pittsburgh NL, 1929
25 Wes Ferrell, Bos./Wash. AL, 1937

Highest Slugging Percentage
.632 Don Newcombe, Brooklyn NL, 1955
.621 Wes Ferrell, Cleveland AL, 1931
.582 Mike Hampton, Colorado NL, 2001
.582 Red Ruffing, Bos./N.Y. AL, 1930
.577 Walter Johnson, Senators AL, 1925
.576 Babe Ruth, Boston AL, 1915
.573 Jack Bentley, New York NL, 1923

To summarize on an overall basis the best season performances since 1900, we have reviewed the various hitting categories and have come up with the following chronological compilation.

Year	Pitcher	G	AB	R	H	2B	3B	HR	RBI	AVG	SLG
1911	Jack Coombs, Phil. AL	52	141	31*	45	6	1	2	23	.319	.418
1912	Claude Hendrix, Pit. NL	39	121	25	39	10	6	1	15	.322	.529
1915	Babe Ruth, Bos. AL	42	92	16	29	10	1	4	21	.315	.576
1921	Carl Mays, N.Y. AL	51	143	18	49	5	1	2	22	.343	.434
1922	Elam Vangilder, StL. AL	45	93	16	32	10	2	2	11	.344	.559
1923	Jack Bentley, N.Y. NL	52	89	9	38	6	2	1	14	.427	.573
1923	George Uhle, Clev. AL	58	144	23	52*	10	3	0	22	.361	.472
1925	Walter Johnson, Wash. AL	36	97	12	42	6	1	2	20	.433*	.577
1930	Ervin Brame, Pit. NL	50	116	20	41	5	0	3	22	.353	.474
1930	Red Ruffing, Bos./N.Y. AL	58	110	17	40	8	2	4	22	.364	.582
1931	Wes Ferrell, Clev. AL	48	116	24	37	6	1	9*	30	.319	.621
1935	Wes Ferrell, Bos. AL	75	150	25	52*	5	1	7	32*	.347	.533
1935	Lynwood Rowe, Det. AL	45	109	19	34	3	2	3	28	.312	.459
1937	Lynn Nelson, Phil. AL	68	90	13	30	2	1	3	26	.333	.478
1939	Curt Davis, StL. NL	63	105	10	40	5	0	1	17	.381	.457
1955	Don Newcombe, Bkn. NL	57	117	18	42	9	1	7	18	.359	.632
1965	Don Drysdale, L.A. NL	58	130	18	39	4	1	7	19	.300	.508
2001	Mike Hampton, COL NL	43	79	20	23	2	0	7	16	.291	.582
2007	Micah Owings, ARI NL	35	60	9	20	7	1	4	15	.333	.683

*Modern Major League record for hurlers.

CAREER BATTING RECORDS

Career records are the ultimate extension of game and season performances and many of the names which surfaced in the earlier chapters will appear here as well. One name that has not been mentioned specifically is Cy Young. He was not a particularly good hitter, but because of his extremely long and active career he automatically established a number of career records that will probably never be broken.

Young, who split his long career evenly in the 19th and 20th centuries, had by far the most at-bats as a pitcher, 2947, the most hits, 618, the most runs, 322, and unofficially the most runs batted in with 289. In spite of his large number of hits, he trailed Red Ruffing in doubles, 97 to 86, Walter Johnson in triples, 41 to 34, and Wes Ferrell and many others in home runs, 38 to 18. Old Cy played five games at first base in which he collected four hits in 11 trips, one a triple. He scored three runs and knocked in one. His batting average as a pitcher was .210.

If the career records were restricted to the 20th century, Walter Johnson would lead in most cumulative categories, except for doubles, homers, and runs batted in. Ruffing had 273 RBIs, one for each of his 273 career pitching victories. Early Wynn was the pitcher to receive the most bases on balls, 141. He was a switch-hitter. As a pitcher he gave up the most walks, 1775, so he was probably trying to get some of those back.

On batting average, we make a concession to the relief pitchers and those with short careers by including the hurlers with 200 to 500 at-bats. Under this listing three hurlers topped the .300 mark Jack Bentley with .322, Ervin Brame, .306, and Babe Ruth, .304. They all batted left-handed. Ironically, one other on the limited at-bat list is Johnny Cooney, who was one of those unusual players who threw left and batted right. He later became

an outfielder who played to an advanced age.
In the longer service category since 1900, the list is topped by
George Uhle, .288, followed by Doc Crandall, .284, Red Lucas,
.282, and Wes Ferrell, .280. See below.

Highest Career Batting Average Since 1900

200 to 500 At-Bats

Career	Bat	Pitcher	H	AB	AVG
1913-27	L	Jack Bentley	109	339	.322
1928-32	L	Ervin Brame	121	396	.306
1914-33	L	Babe Ruth	149	490	.304
1901-04	L	Mike O'Neill	76	260	.292
1919-30	L	Bill Bayne	62	214	.290
1921-30	R	Johnny Cooney	68	236	.288
1929-36	L	Chad Kimsey	58	206	.282
1911-18	L	Earl Yingling	64	227	.282
1901-03	R	Lew Wiltse	62	221	.281

500+ At-Bats

Career	Bat	Pitcher	H	AB	AVG
1919-36	R	George Uhle	393	1363	.288
1908-18	R	Doc Crandall	163	573	.284
1923-38	L	Red Lucas	392	1388	.282
1927-41	R	Wes Ferrell	316	1128	.280
1895-1909	L	Al Orth	389	1400	.278
1916-29	L	Jack Scott	186	678	.274
1949-60	R	Don Newcombe	238	878	.271
1923-33	R	Hollis Thurston	175	648	.270
1924-47	R	Red Ruffing	520	1932	.269
1915-29	L	Carl Mays	291	1085	.268
1894-1903	R	Jim Callahan	181	682	.265
1933-39	L	John Marcum	141	533	.265
1902-15	R	George Mullin	397	1504	.264
1933-49	R	Lynwood Rowe	239	909	.263
1939-53	L	Fred Hutchinson	171	649	.263
1894-1911	B	Jesse Tannehill	285	1093	.261
1922-34	L	Joe Shaute	170	657	.259
1917-27	L	Dutch Ruether	245	947	.259

The list of career home run leaders shows a ladder arrangement with all the top rungs taken. Wes Ferrell had 38 round-trippers, Bob Lemon 37, Red Ruffing 36, and Warren Spahn and Earl Wilson 35. It then drops off to 29 for Don Drysdale, and 24 for three hurlers whose careers spanned much of the last 100 years John Clarkson (1882–94), the early leader, Walter Johnson (1907–27), who led in the middle years, and Bob Gibson (1959–75), who led in the 1960s and '70s.

Although Ferrell and Lemon had the highest totals, neither had the best ratio of home runs to at-bats. Jack Harshman hit four-baggers most frequently in his brief career, followed by Earl Wilson and by Babe Ruth, who just squeezed on the list of hurlers hitting 15 or more. The at-bats are carried as a guide to frequency. The career batting average is also shown to indicate that pitchers are not immune from swinging for the fences. Maybe they have a natural inclination to want to put the ball out of the park so they won't have to rush around the bases.

All those hurlers who have hit 15 or more career homers as a pitcher or pinch-hitter since 1876 are listed here.

Pitcher	HR	AB	AVG
Wes Ferrell	38	1128	.280
Bob Lemon	37	1126	.234
Red Ruffing	36	1932	.269
Warren Spahn	35	1872	.194
Earl Wilson	35	740	.195
Don Drysdale	29	1169	.187
Walter Johnson	24	2288	.237
John Clarkson	24	1895	.218
Bob Gibson	24	1328	.206
Carlos Zambrano	23	659	.241
Jack Stivetts	21	1287	.297
Dizzy Trout	20	961	.213
Milt Pappas	20	1073	.123
Jack Harshman	19	384	.182
Gary Peters	19	807	.222
Cy Young	18	2947	.210
Lynwood Rowe	18	909	.263
Jim Tobin	17	794	.230
Early Wynn	17	1704	.214
Mike Hampton	16	725	.246
Jim Kaat	16	1251	.185
Lefty Grove	15	1369	.148
Jouett Meekin	15	1078	.243
Babe Ruth	15	490	.304
Hal Schumacher	15	893	.202
Claude Passeau	15	982	.192
Joe Nuxhall	15	766	.198
John Antonelli	15	697	.178
Don Newcombe	15	878	.271
Pedro Ramos	15	703	.157
Dick Donovan	15	694	.163
Don Cardwell	15	698	.135
Jim Kaat	15	1191	.189
Rick Wise	15	585	.207

Pitchers who hit home runs seem to have little in common with those who hit for a good average. This is reflected in the two lists carried above where only four names Ferrell, Ruffing, Rowe and Newcombe appear on both lists. Spahn and Wilson, who both hit 35 homers, and Drysdale, who hit 29, all hit under .200. Milt Pappas, who hit 20 homers, batted only .123.

One way to obtain the best combination of power and average is to focus on slugging percentage, which relates at-bats to total bases rather than to hits. Does this give too much weight to the home run hitter? Not for pitchers. Spahn and Drysdale did not even make the list of top sluggers because their low batting averages dragged them out of contention. On the other hand it accentuates the importance of a player like Ferrell who kept his batting average up while still hitting the long ball. He compiled a .451 slugging percentage as a pitcher, comfortably ahead of the other pitchers of the 20th century.

Most of the best hitting pitchers since 1900 are listed below with their career records in the important departments. Only those hurlers with more than 500 at-bats are listed, and they are ranked by slugging percentage.

Pitcher	AB	R	H	2B	3B	HR	RBI	AVG	SLG
Wes Ferrell	1128	169	316	55	12	38*	202	.280	.451*
Doc Crandall	573	77	163	23	15	8	91	.284	.419
Carlos Zambrano	659	72	159	26	3	23	69	.241	.395
Bob Lemon	1126	145	263	52	9	37	146	.234	.394
Red Ruffing	1932	207	520	97*	13	36	273	.269	.389
George Uhle	1363	172	393	60	21	9	187	.288*	.383
Hollis Thurston	648	65	175	38	10	5	79	.270	.383
Lynwood Rowe	909	116	239	36	9	18	153	.263	.382
Al Orth	1400	166	389	54	28	11	184	.278	.380
Tommy Byrne	601	73	143	26	8	14	98	.238	.378
Don Larsen	591	65	144	25	5	14	72	.244	.374
Earl Wilson	740	95	144	12	6	35	111	.195	.369
Don Newcombe	878	94	238	33	3	15	108	.271	.367
Claude Hendrix	921	118	221	39	17	13	97	.240	.362
Mike Hampton	725	97	178	22	5	16	79	.246	.356
Jack Scott	678	67	186	31	4	5	73	.274	.354
Red Lucas	1388	150	392	60	13	3	183	.282	.351
Carl Mays	1085	113	291	32	21	5	110	.268	.350
Gary Peters	807	86	179	31	7	19	102	.222	.348
Mickey McDermott	615	70	154	29	2	9	74	.250	.348
George Mullin	1504	162	397	70	23	3	135	.264	.347
Walter Johnson	2288	234	542	93	41*	24	252	.237	.345

* Modern career record for a pitcher.

Red Lucas   Gary Peters

PITCHERS AS PINCH-HITTERS

Pitchers were among the first pinch-hitters used in 1891 when they were first officially allowed. Bob Caruthers and Jack Stivetts made their initial efforts that season. On June 28, 1894, when Stivetts was with Boston, he went to the plate for Kid Nichols in the ninth with Boston trailing St. Louis 10–7. The Boston Strong Boy belted a home run with two on to tie the game. He then went in to pitch and Boston won in the 10th 11–10. It was only the second major league pinch homer. He went on to hit two more before closing out his career. He also hit a pinch triple on August 15, 1895.

Pitchers used most frequently as pinch-hitters at the turn of the 20th century were Jim Callahan, Mike O'Neill, George Mullin, Jesse Tannehill, Al Orth, and Frank Kitson. There was one game on July 17, 1901, when Vic Willis was pitching for the Boston Braves, where two other Boston hurlers were called off the bench to pinch-hit in the ninth inning. Kid Nichols hit a triple and Bill Dinneen scored him with a single.

Later, when pinch-hitting became a more common practice, several hurlers led all substitute batsmen in season pinch-hitting average. Examples include Frank Lange of the White Sox in 1911, who had 8 hits in 19 trips; Clarence Mitchell, 6-for-18 in 1920; Jack Bentley, 10-for-20 in 1923; George Uhle, 11-for-26 in 1924; Ervin Brame, 10-for-21 in 1930; Red Ruffing, 8-for-18 in 1935; and Chubby Dean, 10-for-26 in 1939.

Red Lucas never led in batting average, but he led four times in hits and three times in appearances. When he concluded his career in 1938, he was by far the most used pinch-hitter in baseball. His career record of 114 pinch hits would stand for almost 30 years until Smoky Burgess became almost exclusively a pinch-hitter with the White Sox in 1965–67. Lucas' career pinch-hitting average was

not all that high. His 114 hits came in 437 official at-bats for a
.261 mark, but his average was eroded by many more appearances
than any other pitcher. The accompanying table shows that he hit
better than any of the top six most active pitcher pinch-hitters.

A detailed analysis of one of these pitcher pinch-hitters might
be of interest to the reader. Red Ruffing was not as active as Red
Lucas, but did have a longer career. He started as a substitute hitter in 1927 when he was with the Red Sox and reached the heights
as a hitter (as well as a pitcher) after he was sold to the Yankees in
1930. The full list of Ruffing's 255 plate appearances as a pinch-
hitter have been compiled by Raymond Gonzalez of New York. He
lists the players Ruffing batted for, the hurlers he faced, and the
results of his substitute role.

Ruffing pinch-hit mostly for his pitching colleagues, including
relief hurler Johnny Murphy 15 times, Bump Hadley 14, Lefty
Gomez 11, and Walter Brown 10. But Red also batted for such reg-
ular players as Bill Rogell, Lyn Lary, Red Rolfe, Joe Sewell, Dixie
Walker, Frank Crosetti, George Selkirk, Tommy Henrich, and Bill
Dickey. Ruffing batted four times for his batterymate, even though
Dickey was a lifetime .312 hitter. Of course, Dickey batted left, and
Ruffing right. There was one case on September 1, 1930 when
Dickey was scheduled to hit against Lee Roy Mahaffey of the
Athletics. But Connie Mack called in his ace Lefty Grove to face
Dickey. Ruffing was then sent in to bat for Dickey and was retired
by Grove. But that was not typical. In fact, Ruffing faced Grove
more often than any other hurler in his pinch-hitting appearances,
and hit him well five hits in 15 at-bats.

Ruffing practically owned another southpaw, Thornton Lee,
getting five hits off him in eight trips. He got his last pinch hit on
August 8, 1947, an RBI single off Hal Newhouser. He was then 43
years old. The Yankee star also faced numerous good right-handed
pitchers such as Ted Lyons, Wes Ferrell, Mel Harder, and Bob Feller.

Red had a total of 58 hits as a substitute swinger, including six
doubles and two homers. He knocked in 38 runs, but scored only
six himself. He was not a good runner, having lost several toes in

a mining accident, and almost every time he got on as a pinch-hitter he was replaced by a pinch-runner. This included 22 times when he was given a base on balls. His pinch-hit batting average was .258, not spectacular, but above the average for those players with 20 or more pinch hits in their careers.

There were three hurlers who compiled pinch-hit marks over .300, but they were short-service players or had limited activity. Fred Heimach, a journeyman hurler with the Athletics and Yankees, had 20 hits in 52 at-bats for a spectacular .385 average. Ervin Brame, who played at the height of great NL batting seasons (1928–32), was 25 for 70 for .357. Jack Bentley pinch-hit at .301. Bob Lemon was next with .291, a mark considerably higher than his total average of .234.

Here is the list of pitchers who were able to accumulate 20 or more pinch hits in their careers. The records are only for those years where the player was primarily a pitcher.

Pitcher	PH	PH AB	HR	AVG
Red Lucas	114	437	2	.261
Red Ruffing	58	225	2	.258
George Uhle	44	169	1	.260
Ray Caldwell	36	154	2	.234
Dutch Ruether	34	135	0	.252
Wes Ferrell	31	139	1	.223
Bob Lemon	30	103	2	.291
Chubby Dean	30	134	0	.224
Lynwood Rowe	28	101	2	.277
Clarence Mitchell	27	134	2	.201
Mickey McDermott	25	127	2	.197
Jack Bentley	25	83	2	.301
Ervin Brame	25	70	0	.357
Joe Bowman	24	109	1	.220
Walter Johnson	21	110	1	.191
Lynn Nelson	21	89	3	.236
George Mullin	20	101	0	.198
Fred Hutchinson	20	91	1	.220
Don Newcombe	20	87	0	.230
Fred Heimach	20	52	0	.385

Ironically, the pitcher who hit the most pinch homers is not on the list of those who collected 20 pinch hits. This is Gary Peters, a left-handed swinger who had 16 hits in 66 pinch-hit at-bats, and four of those hits were for the distance. His first, on July 19, 1964, came in the 13th inning and gave the White Sox a 3–2 win over Kansas City.

Lynn Nelson was the only other pitcher to hit as many as three pinch homers, two for the A's and one for the Tigers. As mentioned earlier, Jack Stivetts hit three in the 1890s, but the second, on September 16, 1897, and the third, on June 9, 1898, came when he was actually playing more games at other positions. Consequently, it would not be correct, according to our own rules, to call them pinch homers by a pitcher.

The full list, bearing many repeaters and including five pitchers who hit pinch slams, is carried below.

Jack Stivetts, Bos. NL June 28, 1894
Mike O'Neill, StL. NL June 3, 1902 (Slam)
Doc White, Phil. NL September 19, 1902
Ray Caldwell, NY AL June 10, 1915
Ray Caldwell, NY AL June 11, 1915
Claude Hendrix, Chi. FL June 17, 1915
Babe Ruth, Bos. AL June 12, 1916
Clarence Mitchell, Bkn NL June 24, 1919 (1)
Jimmy Zinn, Phi. AL September 15, 1919
Willie Sherdel, StL. NL April 20, 1920
Clarence Mitchell. Bkn NL May 29, 1922
Jack Bentley, NY NL August 26, 1923
George Uhle, Clev. AL August 19, 1924
Joe Bush, NY AL September 18, 1924
Walter Johnson, Wash. AL May 19, 1925
Hal Carson, Phi. NL May 30, 1925
Jack Bentley, NY NL August 24, 1925
Charlie Barnabe, Chi. AL May 1, 1928
Red Ruffing, Bos. AL September 2, 1929

Red Lucas, Cin. NL September 20, 1930 (2)
Chad Kimsey, StL AL July 7, 1931
Clise Dudley, Phil. NL August 6, 1932 (1)
Red Lucas, Cin. NL May 27, 1933
John Marcum, Phil. AL September 12, 1934
Ralph Winegarner, Clev. AL June 20, 1935
Wes Ferrell, Bos. AL June 21, 1935
Red Ruffing, NY AL June 5, 1937
Lynn Nelson, Phil. AL August 1, 1937 (1)
Lynn Nelson, Phil. AL August 20, 1937
Joe Bowman, Pitt. NL April 26, 1940
Lynn Nelson, Det. AL June 21, 1940
Charlie Frye, Phi. NL August 21, 1940
Jim Tobin, Bos. NL May 12, 1942
Lynwood Rowe, Phil. NL May 2, 1943 (Slam)
Lynwood Rowe, Phil. NL July 4, 1943 (2)
Zeb Eaton, Det. AL July 15, 1945 (Slam)
Zeb Eaton, Det. AL August 8, 1945 (2)
Early Wynn, Wash. AL September 15, 1946 (Slam)
Early Wynn, Wash. AL July 5, 1947
Fred Hutchinson, Det. AL August 13, 1947
Carl Scheib, Phil. AL August 29, 1948 (2)
Bob Lemon, Clev. AL April 23, 1950
Tommy Byrne, Chi. AL May 16, 1953 (Slam)
Johnny Lindell, Pitt. NL June 25, 1953
Johnny Lindell, Pitt. NL August 15, 1953
Bob Lemon, Clev. AL July 8, 1956
Maury McDermott, KC AL August 10, 1957
Maury McDermott, KC AL August 14, 1957
Tommy Byrne, NY AL September 15, 1957 (1)
Don Larsen, NY AL August 17, 1958
Don Larsen, KC AL May 22, 1961
Gary Peters, Chi. AL July 19, 1964 (1) 13th inn.
Earl Wilson, Det. AL July 15, 1966 13th inn.
Earl Wilson, Det. AL May 13, 1967

Gary Peters, Chi. AL August 11, 1968 (1)
Gary Peters, Bos. AL August 22, 1971 (1)
Gary Peters, Bos. AL September 4, 1971
Don Robinson, SFG NL June 19, 1990
Omar Olivares, PHI NL July 24, 1995
Gene Stechschulte, STL NL April 17, 2001
Brooks Kieschnick, MIL NL June 15, 2003 (as DH)
Brooks Kieschnick, MIL NL June 25, 2003 10th inn.
Brooks Kieschnick, MIL NL June 27, 2003 (as DH)
Brooks Kieschnick, MIL NL September 17, 2003
Brooks Kieschnick, MIL NL April 22, 2004
Micah Owings, ARI NL April 30, 2008
Micah Owings, CIN NL May 10, 2009

BASESTEALING BY PITCHERS

Pitchers are not expected to steal bases and they seldom do these days. There was a little spurt of activity when Bob Gibson stole five bases for the Cardinals during the 1969 season, and John "Blue Moon" Odom, used frequently as a pinch-runner for the Oakland A's, swiped four bases in 1972. This still does not compare with some of the base-stealing exploits of pitchers in the first part of this century.

There have been three examples of pitchers stealing three bases in one game since 1900, and each involved a steal of home. The American League was in its first season on August 10, 1901 when Win Mercer of Washington beat Connie Mack's Philadelphia Athletics 10–4 in the first game of a twin bill. Mercer collected only one hit, but got on twice by other means and stole both times. In addition, he was on the scoring end of a double steal in the fourth inning. Stealing three bases was quite a trick for a pitcher, but getting four extra-base hits in a game was even more unusual and that was accomplished by Lew Wiltse of the A's, who shut out the Senators 13–0 in the second game of that double-header. He banged out two doubles and two triples to steal the limelight from Mercer.

Another record-book performance took place on July 14, 1915, but a closer look reveals that it wouldn't even be included under present playing conditions.

On that day the White Sox were leading the Philadelphia A's 4–2 in the fourth inning when rain threatened. A's hurler Bullet Joe Bush tried to delay the game by walking White Sox batters. One of his stray tosses hit pitcher Red Faber, who was at the plate. Faber took first, and then in an effort to get thrown out (to speed up the game) he continued running to second, third, and home. The A's in turn made only a half-hearted effort to throw him out. In spite of this sorry exhibition, the record book credits Faber with three steals in one inning. Ironically, his "steal" of home turned out to be the winning run as the threatened rain never materialized and the White Sox won 6–4.

The Faber frolic should not be confused with the dazzling performance of Wild Bill Donovan of Detroit in a game against Cleveland on May 7, 1906. Donovan singled in the fifth inning, stole second and third (while Ty Cobb fanned), and then home on a double steal. He also hit a triple and won an 8–3 victory. Donovan also stole home against Cleveland on September 14, 1905 en route to a shutout victory.

Donovan was probably the best basestealer among pitchers since 1900. He even stole a base against the Cubs in the 1908 World Series, the only hurler to so distinguish himself in the Fall Classic. On a career basis he had 30 steals as a hurler, compared to 28 for Bill Dinneen. Ray Caldwell, who came along a decade later, had 20. Burleigh Grimes, 1916–34, had 15. Rip Sewell had 12 when he quit in 1949, and Bob Gibson had 13 when he closed out his career in 1975. Thirteen steals may not seem like a large number until you realize that several regular players who were contemporaries had fewer. Dal Maxvill had a career total of 7, Frank Howard 8, Rico Petrocelli 10, and Deron Johnson 11. Among players from the 1970s, Richie Zisk finished his career with just 8.

The pitcher to steal the most bases in a season was Jim Callahan of the White Sox in 1901. He swiped nine that season while Bill Dinneen had eight for the Boston Braves. When Callahan converted to a full-time performer, he had some good theft totals, including 45 in 1911 when he was 37 years old. Donovan had six steals in 1906 and after that the scason totals started to go down. Wilbur Cooper had five with the Pirates in 1919, and Howard Ehmke had four with the Red Sox in 1924. Then for many years in the batting era of the 1920s and 1930s, no hurler stole more than two in a season. Therefore, it came as a shock in 1943 when Rip Sewell of the Pirates stole seven in a year when the Pirate leader had 12 and Arky Vaughan led the league with 20.

The only high marks after that were five by Gibson in 1969 and four by Odom in 1972. The latter was used 28 times as a pinch-runner that season, and more than 100 times in his short career. The only other hurler used that much on a career basis was Pedro Ramos. He gained the reputation as a very fast runner back in the 1950s, partly because he kept challenging Mickey Mantle to a race (which never came off). Although admittedly very quick on his feet, Ramos had only two career steals. Another Latin player, Ruben Gomez, also had only two career steals although used frequently as a pinch-runner. As a rookie in 1953 he was used 32 times compared to 29 as a pitcher.

Pitchers probably have shown off best while stealing home. They have done it a remarkable number of times, at least in the early days of the 20th century. Surprisingly, eight hurlers have done it twice; however, it hasn't been done at all since 1955.

On May 26, 1955, Don Newcombe of the Brooklyn Dodgers went into the ninth of a close game with the Pirates. With two runners on base, the big hurler, who was one of the best hitting pitchers in the game, hit a long fly ball which was misjudged by the outfielder and fell for a triple. Normally a pitcher would be gasping for breath at that point, but while El Roy Face was getting ready to deliver to the next batter, Newcombe lumbered home. Face, caught flat-footed, threw wildly, almost hitting Don, who slid in safely. Newcombe won the game 6–2 over Face, who pitched the route one of the few times in his career. Newcombe's was the last of 36 steals of home by a pitcher since 1900.

Almost all of the pitcher steals of home were double steals where a teammate was advancing to second. There were only four individual thefts, including that of Newcombe, which merit some attention.

On August 8, 1903, Joe McGinnity was pitching one of his famous doubleheader victories. He had beaten the Dodgers 6–1 in the opener. In the third inning of the second game he singled, went to second on a sacrifice, and when the throw was bad he went on to third, which he made on a disputed call by the umpire.

While the Dodgers were arguing, Joe dashed home. Dodger hurler Henry Schmidt was so angry he threw the ball out of the park. For this he was banished from the game.

On April 20, 1946, Bucky Walters of the Reds was hooked up in a pitchers battle with Rip Sewell of the Pirates. In the sixth, Walters bunted safely. He moved to third on a sacrifice and a ground out, and with two strikes on Grady Hatton, Walters caught Sewell napping and stole home. It was the only run off Sewell who beat Bucky 2–1 before 28,000 at Pittsburgh.

Fred Hutchinson of Detroit was a real hero on August 29, 1947 when he tripled against the Browns in the third, and when Ellis Kinder took a big windup, he hustled home in front of the throw. Hutch also singled and won the game 5–4.

The only pitcher to steal home in extra innings was George Mogridge of Washington. This took place in the 12th inning of a tie game against the White Sox on August 15, 1923. Mogridge worked a double steal with Nemo Liebold to provide one of the insurance runs in a 5–1 victory over Charles Robertson.

Here is a rundown on those pitchers who stole home in major league games since 1900.

National League Hurlers Stealing Home Since 1900

Date	Basestealer and Club	Inn.	Opponent
July 15, 1902	John Menefee, Chicago	5	Brooklyn
August 8, 1903 (2)	Joe McGinnity, N.Y.	3	Brooklyn
April 29, 1904	Joe McGinnity, N.Y.	7	Boston
September 12, 1911 (2)	Christy Mathewson, N.Y.	3	Boston
May 22, 1912	Leon Ames, N.Y.	5	Brooklyn
June 28, 1912	Christy Mathewson, N.Y.	4	Boston
July 22, 1913	Slim Salee, N.Y.	3	St. Louis
April 19, 1916	Sherry Smith, Brooklyn	3	New York
June 23, 1916	Tom Seaton, Chicago	5	Cincinnati
July 26, 1918	Robert Steele, N.Y.	7	St. Louis
August 9, 1919	Jim Vaughn, Chicago	8	New York
September 3, 1919	Dutch Ruether, Cin.	4	Chicago
July 27, 1920	Jesse Bames, N.Y.	6	St. Louis
May 4, 1921	Dutch Ruether, Brooklyn	5	New York
September 23, 1943	John Vander Meer, Cin.	5	New York
April 20, 1946	Bucky Walters, Cin.	6	Pittsburgh
May 26, 1955	Don Newcombe, Brooklyn	9	Pittsburgh

American League Hurlers Stealing Home

Date	Basestealer and Club	Inn.	Opponent
August 10, 1901	Win Mercer, Washington	4	Philadelphia
August 2, 1904	Frank Owen, Chicago	3	Washington
September 14, 1905	Bill Donovan, Detroit	4	Cleveland
May 7, 1906	Bill Donovan, Detroit	5	Cleveland
April 27, 1908	Frank Owen, Chicago	9	St. Louis
June 13, 1908	Ed Walsh, Chicago	7	New York
July 2, 1909	Ed Walsh, Chicago	6	St. Louis
August 30, 1909	Eddie Plank, Phil.	2	Chicago
August 27, 1910 (1)	Jack Warhop, New York	6	Chicago
July 12, 1912	Jack Warhop, New York	3	St. Louis
July 14, 1915	Urban Faber, Chicago	4	Philadelphia
August 7, 1916	Reb Russell, Chicago	3	Boston
August 24, 1918	Babe Ruth, Boston	2	St. Louis
July 8, 1921	Dickie Kerr, Chicago	7	New York
April 23, 1923	Urban Faber, Chicago	4	St. Louis
August 15, 1923	George Mogridge, Wash.	12	Chicago
September 17, 1944	Joe Haynes, Chicago	8	St. Louis
August 29, 1947	Fred Hutchinson, Detroit	3	St. Louis
June 2, 1950 (2)	Harry Dorish, St. Louis	5	Washington

Bill Donovan, one of the best basestealers among pitchers, shown here as playing manager of the New York Yankees in 1915.

ADVENT OF THE
DESIGNATED HITTER RULE

Batting in the 1960s reached a pretty low level of achievement. The American League in 1968 came close to having a batting champion hitting under .300. Fortunately Carl Yastrzemski was able to get his finger tips over that coveted standard and finish at .301. Batting by pitchers suffered the same decline and some led the majors with batting averages as low as .241, .242, and .243. But this decline had already been taking place on a gradual basis.

Pete Palmer has done an analysis of batting by pitchers in two American League seasons which were typical of different eras 1927 and 1960. The latter season was just before the Junior Circuit expanded its number of teams and number of games, so there is an even basis of comparison. In 1927 the AL batted at a level of .285. The pitchers batted at .208, which was 77 points lower. In 1960 the league batting average was .255 while the pitchers batted at .155, exactly 100 points lower. Here is a further comparison in different categories.

This decline is reflected in the all-time listing of pitchers who were most inept at the plate. Almost all of them played in the 1960s. Of course, many of the poorest hitters were relief hurlers who did not have much opportunity or inclination to develop batting skills. There is the extreme example of Fred Gladding, who, in his 13 years as a fireman, had only one hit in 63 at-bats for an .016 lifetime average. Ron Herbel, in 206 career at-bats from 1963 to 1971, collected only a half dozen hits for a .029 lifetime average.

In regard to the longer service or more active hurlers, we show below those with the lowest career batting averages in more than 400 at-bats since 1900.

Pitcher Batting, 1927 vs 1960   Lowest Pitcher AVG (min. 400 AB)

1927	Stat	1960
3665	AB	3053
321	Runs	234
761	Hits	473
1012	TB	584
120	2B	65
25	3B	5
27	HR	12
248	SH	250
7	SB	4
183	BB	229
751	SO	946
335	RBI	192
16	HBP	8
.208	BA	.155

Period	Pitcher	H	AB	AVG
1961-71	Dean Chance	44	662	.066
1965-75	Bill Hands	37	472	.078
1955-66	Roger Craig	38	448	.085
1958-71	Dick Ellsworth	59	673	.088
1952-72	Hoyt Wilhelm	38	432	.088
1953-67	Bob Buhl	76	857	.089
1956-71	George Brunet	37	418	.089
1952-70	Ron Kline	45	491	.092
1969-76	Clay Kirby	47	488	.096
1955-66	Sandy Koufax	75	776	.097
1934-52	Al Benton	50	512	.098

Because of the general deterioration in batting by pitchers, the International League in 1969 experimented with a system whereby a team could use a designated hitter for a pitcher. Some managers claimed they disliked the idea but, even though the DH was optional, all used it. Based on minor league experience, discussion then centered on possible adoption of this rule change at the major league level. Commissioner Bowie Kuhn, who for several years had insisted that batting averages ought to be higher, favored adoption of the DH. The National League refused to go along with the idea. The American League decided to adopt it on an experimental basis starting with the 1973 season.

There was much speculation about whether all clubs would use this opportunity to beef up their attack or would still go with some of their better hitting hurlers. A review of the top hitters at the close of the 1972 season (in both leagues) indicates the following career records for those with more than 200 at-bats.

Pitcher	AB	R	H	2B	3B	HR	RBI	SB	AVG
Jim Hunter	656	60	148	16	3	6	51	1	.226
Gary Peters	807	86	179	31	7	19	102	0	.222
Dave Roberts	227	21	48	4	0	4	18	0	.211
Rick Wise	497	46	104	15	4	12	47	0	.209
Bob Gibson	1154	117	240	40	4	22	126	12	.208
Juan Pizarro	648	72	131	18	2	8	64	1	.202
John Odom	391	59	78	8	2	12	30	5	.199
Jim Perry	889	73	177	22	3	5	59	0	.199
Tony Cloninger	621	65	119	16	2	11	67	1	.192
Jim Kaat	1010	98	193	35	4	14	88	4	.191
Claude Osteen	968	82	182	26	6	8	72	2	.188
Ray Sadecki	716	55	134	18	4	5	51	0	.187

American League managers essentially accepted the Designated Hitter concept from the first day of the 1973 season. By design or accident, a few pitchers got a chance to hit. Ken Brett of the White Sox was allowed to hit 12 times in 1976. He did get one single, but was still responsible for a dozen outs since he hit into one double play.

Here is a list of the American League pitchers who batted in the period 1973 through 1994 (interleague play began in 1995). The cumulative result in 106 plate appearances and 98 at-bats is eight hits, including one double and one triple, three runs scored and three RBI, two walks, two sacrifice flies, and three sacrifice bunts.

1973
Lindy McDaniel, NY twice (two strikeouts)
Cy Acosta, Chi. once (strikeout)
Vida Blue, Oak. once (out)
Rollie Fingers, Oak. once (strikeout)
Terry Forster, Chi. once (out)
Ken Holtzman, Oak. once (base on balls)
Jim "Catfish" Hunter, Oak. once (single)
Darold Knowles, Oak. once (sacrifice fly, RBI)

John "Blue Moon" Odom, Oak. once (out, also scored 5 runs as pinch-runner)
Ed Rodriguez, Mil. once (triple, run)
Chris Short, Mil. once (catcher's interference)

1974
Cy Acosta, Chi. twice (two strikeouts)
Ferguson Jenkins, Texas twice (single, run, strikeout)
Tom Murphy, Mil. twice (single, out)
Joe Henderson, Chi. once (out)
Jim Kaat, Chi. once (out)
Sparky Lyle, NY once (out)
Ken Tatum, Chi. once (out, reached on error)

1975
Ken Holtzman, Oak. twice (two outs)
Vic Albury, Minn. once (strikeout)
Stan Bahnsen, Oak. once (strikeout)
Bill Campbell, Minn. once (strikeout)
Rollie Fingers, Oak. once (out)
Paul Lindblad, Oak. once (out)
Steve Mingori, K.C. once (strikeout)
Sonny Siebert, Oak. once (strikeout)
Luis Tiant, Bos. once (out)

1976
Ken Brett, Chi. 12 times (single, K, DP, 9 other outs)
Frank MacCormack, Det. 3 times (two strikeouts, out)
John Hiller, Det. once (out)
Catfish Hunter, NY once (out)
Mark Littell, K.C. once (strikeout)
Dick Pole, Bos. once (out)
Luis Tiant, Bos. once (strikeout)
Jim Willoughby, Bos. once (out)

1977
Vida Blue, Oak. once (strikeout)
Mark Littell, K.C. once (strikeout)
Jim Norris, Oak. once (strikeout)

1978
Jim Kern, Clev. once (strikeout)

1979
Ron Davis, NY once (strikeout)
Joel Finch, Bos. once (out)
Dave Heaverlo, Oak. once (out)
Bill Travers, Mil. once (sacrifice bunt)

Ken Brett, who went to bat 12 times as an American League hurler in 1976, when the DH was in force. At the time he was the leading batter among hurlers with 200 or more career at-bats. His batting average is .262 (91 hits in 347 at-bats).

1980
Ron Davis, NYY once (strikeout)
Dick Drago, BOS once (out)
Dave Stieb, TOR once (out)

1981
None

1982
Rick Langford, OAK once (out)

1983
Jamie Easterly, MIL twice (sacrifice bunt, out)
Keith Atherton, OAK once (strikeout)

1984
Floyd Bannister, CHW once (out)
Bill Caudill, OAK once (strikeout)
Ron Reed, CHW once (out)

1985
Willie Hernandez, DET once (out)
Tim Lollar, BOS once (out)
Gene Nelson, CHW once (out)
Dan Spillner, CHW once (base on balls)
Rick Waits, MIL once (strikeout)

1986
Bill Dawley, CHW twice (two outs)
Ray Fontenot, MIN once (strikeout)
Tim Lollar, BOS once (single)

1987
Mike Henneman, DET once (strikeout)
Mike Moore, SEA once (out)

Jack Morris, DET once (out)
Bobby Witt, TEX once (strikeout)
Curt Young, OAK once (out)

1988
Rick Rhoden, NYY twice (sacrifice fly, RBI, out)
Jeff Russell, TEX once (out)

1989
Allan Anderson, MIN once (strikeout)

1990
Rick Honeycutt, OAK twice (strikeout, out)
Kevin Brown, TEX once (out)
Brian Holman, SEA once (out)
Mike Schooler, SEA once (out)

1991
Bill Gullickson, DET once (sacrifice bunt)
Mike Jeffcoat, TEX once (double, run, RBI)
Frank Tanana, DET once (strikeout)

1992
Mark Langston, CAL twice (two strikeouts, also scored run as
pinch-runner)

1993
Jeff Bronkey, TEX once (out)
Matt Maysey, MIL once (single)
Gregg Olson, BAL once (strikeout)
Jesse Orosco, MIL once (strikeout)

1994
Ron Darling, OAK once (out)
Doug Henry, MIL once (strikeout)
Bob Welch, OAK once (out)

BATTING BY PITCHERS IN THE WORLD SERIES

Although there have been flashes of hitting ability by hurlers in World Series games, no hurler had sustained superior performance at bat. Ken Holtzman had a homer and double in four trips for Oakland in 1974, which was the second year of the DH in regular season play in the American League. That gave him four extra-base hits in World Series play, the most of any pitcher, and a career slugging percentage of .833.

Jack Bentley had the best batting average .417 on five hits in 12 trips. Dutch Ruether hit two triples and also batted .364 in seven World Series games. Dave McNally of the Orioles collected only two hits in 16 trips, but both were home runs. One was a grand slam, giving him a total of six runs batted in. Even Babe Ruth had only one hit in 11 at-bats while pitching in the Series for the Red Sox. Red Ruffing could collect only six hits in 34 trips. This included three at-bats as a pinch-hitter, which itself is quite a compliment for a Series pitcher.

Here is a list of some of the more productive batters, including those with long service, among World Series hurlers. The cumulative records include only those with more than 10 at-bats.

Pitcher	G	AB	R	H	2B	3B	HR	RBI	AVG	SLG
Jack Bentley	10	12	1	5	1	0	1	2	.417	.750
Dutch Ruether	7	11	2	4	1	2*	0	4	.364	.818
Ken Holtzman	8	12	4*	4	3*	0	1	1	.333	.833*
Jack Coombs	6	24	1	8	1	0	0	4	.333	.375
Dizzy Dean	6	15	3	5	2	0	0	1	.333	.467
Burleigh Grimes	9	19	1	6	0	0	0	2	.316	.316
Johnny Podres	7	16	2	5	1	0	0	1	.313	.375
Allie Reynolds	15	26	2	8	1	0	0	2	.308	.346
C. Mathewson	11	32	2	9*	0	0	0	1	.281	.281
Red Ruffing	14	34	1	6	1	0	0	4	.176	.206
Bob Gibson	9	28	4*	4	0	0	2*	3	.143	.357
Dave McNally	9	16	2	2	0	0	2*	6*	.125	.500
Whitey Ford	22*	49*	4*	4	0	0	0	3	.082	.082

Pitchers hitting home runs in World Series games or the League Championship Series are listed below.

World Series
Jim Bagby, Indians, 1920
Rosy Ryan, Giants, 1924
Jack Bentley, Giants, 1924
Jess Haines, Cardinals, 1926
Bucky Walters, Reds, 1940
Lew Burdette, Braves, 1958
Mudcat Grant, Twins, 1965
Jose Santiago, Red Sox, 1967
Bob Gibson, Cardinals, 1967 and 1968
Mickey Lolich, Tigers, 1968
Dave McNally, Orioles, 1969 and 1970 (Slam)
Ken Holtzman, A's, 1974
Joe Blanton, Phillies, 2008

League Championship Series
Mike Cuellar, Orioles, 1970 (Slam)
Don Gullett, Reds, 1975
Steve Carlton, Phillies, 1978
Rick Sutcliffe, Cubs, 1984
Kerry Wood, Cubs, 2003
Jeff Suppan, Cardinals, 2006

League Division Series
None

BATTING BY PITCHERS IN ALL-STAR GAMES

Batting by pitchers in All-Star games has been extremely limited because of their short stints on the mound. This has been particularly true in recent years when all mound appearances were three innings or less and the opportunities to use pinch-hitters were seldom missed. Lefty Gomez pitched six innings in the 1935 game, Mel Harder went five frames in 1934, Al Benton also went five in 1942 when the three-inning limit was lifted, and Larry Jansen and Jim Hunter both pitched five in extra-inning games in 1950 and 1967.

Gomez went to bat the most times, a total of six in five games. He collected only one hit but this was good enough to drive in the first run in All-Star competition in the inaugural game in 1933. He singled in Jimmy Dykes from third in the second inning. No hurler collected more than one hit in All-Star competition. Steve Carlton, Johnny Podres, and Bucky Walters hit doubles, and Lon Warneke hit a triple. Red Ruffing and Vic Raschi each batted in two runs.

Here are the records of the 18 pitchers who achieved a safe hit in All-Star competition.

Pitcher	G	AB	R	H	2B	3B	HR	RBI	AVG
Hank Borowy	1	1	0	1	0	0	0	1	1.000
Steve Carlton	3	2	0	1	1	0	0	1	.500
Murry Dickson	1	1	0	1	0	0	0	1	1.000
Lefty Gomez	5	6	0	1	0	0	0	1	.167
Jack Kramer	1	1	1	1	0	0	0	0	1.000
Emil Leonard	1	1	0	1	0	0	0	0	1.000
Juan Marichal	8	2	1	1	0	0	0	0	.500
Ken McBride	1	1	0	1	0	0	0	1	1.000
Ray Narleski	1	1	0	1	0	0	0	0	1.000
Don Newcombe	4	3	0	1	0	0	0	1	.333
Hal Newhouser	5	3	1	1	0	0	0	0	.333
Bobo Newsom	2	1	0	1	0	0	0	0	1.000
Billy Pierce	4	1	1	1	0	0	0	0	1.000
Johnny Podres	2	1	1	1	1	0	0	0	1.000
Vic Raschi	4	2	0	1	0	0	0	2	.500
Red Ruffing	3	2	0	1	0	0	0	2	.500
Bucky Walters	5	1	1	1	1	0	0	0	1.000
Lon Warneke	3	2	1	1	0	1	0	0	.500

NO-HIT HURLERS AT BAT

How important is hitting to a pitcher? Being more specific, what was Tiger pitcher George Mullin thinking about when he walked to the mound for the ninth inning of his no-hit, no-run game against the Browns on July 4, 1912? He could have had anniversary thoughts because the United States was 136 years old that day and he was 32. But that wasn't it. When Mullin went out to the mound in the top of the ninth he looked back at the press box and held up three fingers. The enthusiastic Detroit crowd probably thought he was indicating that he had but three outs to go for a no-hitter. Instead he was signaling to the scorekeeper that he thought he had three hits his eighth inning single being somewhat questionable and he wanted confirmation. He got that confirmation and then went about the work of retiring the last three Brownies for a 7–0 masterpiece.

How have pitchers performed at bat while pitching a no-hit game? Not too good. The pitchers went hitless in more than half of those games. This is not surprising as most hurlers working on no-hitters are usually more concerned about conserving their energy for pitching and less about hitting. In this context, the performance of Rick Wise on June 23, 1971 was indeed remarkable. He not only pitched a no-hit, no-run game for the Phils against the Reds, but hit two homers and knocked in three runs. The eight total bases were a record for a no-hit hurler.

The best previous effort was by Wes Ferrell, who homered and doubled and knocked in four runs in his 1931 gem for Cleveland. Old Cy Young, in his 1908 no-hit game, knocked in four runs with three singles, and Catfish Hunter sent three runners home with two singles and a double in his perfect game for Oakland in 1968.

In his 1905 no-hitter for the White Sox, Frank Smith got two hits and scored three runs in a 15–0 romp. Bobo Holloman in his "first start" no-hitter for the Browns in 1953 knocked in three runs with two singles. The biggest individual wallop was by Vernon Kennedy for the White Sox in 1935 when he tripled with the bases loaded. Imagine going back to the mound after that type of effort! Jim Tobin in 1944 and Earl Wilson in 1962 both hit solo homers in three trips each. You have to go back to the dark ages to find another no-hit pitcher collecting a four-bagger. It was in the old American Association back in June 1884 when Frank Mountain of the Columbus club connected in Washington.

Here are the records of some of the no-hit hurlers who also performed well at the plate.

Date	Player and Team	AB	R	H	2B	3B	HR	RBI
September 6, 1905	Frank Smith, White Sox	4	3*	2	1	0	0	0
June 30, 1908	Cy Young, Red Sox	4	1	3*	0	0	0	4*
July 4, 1912	George Mullin, Tigers	4	0	3*	1	0	0	2
September 9, 1914	George Davis, Braves	4	1	3*	0	0	0	1
April 29, 1931	Wes Ferrell, Indians	4	2	2	1	0	1	4*
August 13, 1935	Vern Kennedy, White Sox	4	0	1	0	1	0	3
May 6, 1953	Bobo Holoman, Browns	3	0	2	0	0	0	3
May 8, 1968	Jim Hunter, A's	4	0	3*	1	0	0	3
June 23, 1971	Rick Wise, Phillies	4	2	2	0	0	2*	3

PITCHER-BATTER BRIEFS

Fred Gladding pitched short relief in the majors for 13 years. He went to bat only 63 times in that period and collected only one safe hit. What were the circumstances of this earth-shaking achievement and who was the pitcher who so far has escaped the notoriety of giving up this isolated bingle?

The date was July 30, 1969 and the scene was Shea Stadium in New York. Gladding was pitching the last 2 2/3 innings for Houston, which was walloping the Mets in the first game of a twin bill. His single off Ron Taylor came in the middle of an 11-run outburst in the ninth inning. Denis Menke had already hit a grand slam homer off Cal Koonce, and after Taylor came in the Astros gave him the same treatment. Gladding's single scored a run and then Fred rode home on Jimmy Wynn's grand slam, the second home run in the inning. For Taylor, who gained fame for pitching seven hitless innings in four World Series games, this was not one of his good days.

* * * *

On September 12, 1969, the New York Mets had one of those rare achievements where they beat the Pirates 1–0 in both games of a twin bill. Furthermore, the winning pitchers knocked in the only run of each 1–0 victory. In the first contest it was Jerry Koosman, one of baseball's poorest hitters, who singled in the run in the fifth inning. It was his only RBI of the season. In the second game it was Don Cardwell who did the honors by singling in Bud Harrelson.

* * * *

Charles "Hoss" Radbourn, iron-man hurler for Providence in the 1880s, was involved in two unusual shutouts for his club. He was the player who hit a home run in the 18th inning to give Providence a 1–0 thriller over Detroit on August 17, 1882. Actually, he was playing the outfield that day while Monte Ward pitched the full distance for the victory. A year later, on August 21, 1883, Radbourn did take to the mound and blanked Philadelphia 28–0 in the majors' most lopsided shutout. He batted clean-up that day and banged out four hits.

* * * *

Seven pitchers were good enough bunters to lead or tie for leadership in sacrifice hits. Bob Harris of the Browns was the first to achieve this feat in 1941 when he had 14 sacrifice hits to share leadership in the American League with Lou Boudreau and Mike Kreevich. Denny McLain of the Tigers led twice. The full list follows:

> 1941 AL Bob Harris, Browns 14 (co-leader)
> 1948 NL Johnny Sain, Braves 16
> 1968 AL Denny McLain, Tigers 16
> 1968 NL Phil Niekro, Braves 18
> 1969 NL Denny McLain, Tigers 13 (co-leader)
> 1969 NL Jim Meritt, Reds 15
> 1970 NL Pat Dobson. Padres 19

* * * *

Most pitchers are known to be fairly easy strikeout victims at the plate. For example, Wilbur Wood fanned 65 times in 1972, Vida Blue 63 times in 1971, and Dean Chance 63 times in only 93 at-bats in 1968. Chance, who made even Sandy Koufax look adequate as a hitter, whiffed 420 times in 662 career at-bats. His frequency goes unchallenged, although he did not play long enough to have the most career strikeouts. It looked like Milt Pappas might have the mark with 510 lifetime strikeouts, but a review of the K column back in the 1920s and 1930s, when strikeouts were considerably less frequent, indicates that Lefty Grove accumulated a surprising 593 strikeouts from 1925 to 1941. Ironically, his famous battery-mate, Mickey Cochrane, had only 217 lifetime whiffs.

The hurler most difficult to fan was Johnny Sain. He struck out only 20 times in his career of 770 at-bats. Compare that with Chance's 420 in 662 at-bats. Sain went through the entire 1946 season without going down on strikes in 94 at-bats. The next season, in 107 at-bats, he fanned only once. He had a string of 91 consecutive games and 154 at-bats from April 29, 1942, to June 26, 1947 when he did not strike out. In 1972 Sain was the pitching coach for the White Sox when Wilbur Wood set the record for pitchers by striking out 65 times. Maybe Sain should have given Wood a little batting instruction at the same time.

Do pitchers receive intentional walks when batting? The answer is not very frequently, at least not since these statistics were first compiled officially in 1955. Jim Kaat of Minnesota received the last one on September 1, 1970. Gary Peters received one in each of three seasons 1963, 1967, 1968. Don Newcombe had one in 1959 and there were a few other isolated cases. Mickey McDermott received two in one season for Kansas City in 1957. The second one came on September 6, when he pinch-hit for Billy Hunter in the ninth against the White Sox. Dixie Howell, pitching in relief for Chicago, gave him four wide ones and McDermott went to first base, but no further. In the bottom of the ninth, Howell came to bat and since he was not given an intentional base on balls he hit a home run to win his own game 4–3.

Among the intentional walks prior to 1955 there is the case of Red Ruffing batting against the Cleveland Indians on August 5, 1939. He had already hit a home run and a single against Harry Eisenstat, so when Red came up in the seventh with the score tied 1–1, the Indian southpaw put him on base. He was subsequently forced at second by Frank Crosetti and the strategy looked good.

Several hits followed, however, including a home run by Joe DiMaggio, and the Yanks won 6–1.

* * * *

It was stated in an earlier chapter that Scott Stratton was the youngest pitcher to hit a home run when he connected for Louisville in his debut on April 21, 1888. Actually, he was only five days younger than John Montgomery Ward was when the latter hit one for Providence on September 27, 1878. Ward, who later played full-time in the infield and outfield, was then 18 years, 6 months and 24 days. Another 18-year-old pitcher who hit a four-bagger was Larry Dierker of Houston on August 3, 1965.

At the other end of the age spectrum, we have Jack Quinn, pitching for the Athletics on June 27, 1930, and hitting a homer at age 45 years and 11 months. Dazzy Vance, hurling for the Cardinals on September 11, 1934, hit one at age 43 and 6 months; and Warren Spahn of the Milwaukee Braves connected on July 22, 1964 when he was 43 and 3 months.

The youngest American League player ever to collect a hit was pitcher Jim Derrington, bonus baby of the White Sox, who was making his debut on the final day of the 1956 season on September 30. He collected one single in two trips while losing 7–6 to Kansas City. He was 16 years and 10 months at the time, making him also the youngest pitcher to start a game in the majors since 1900.

* * * *

If Terry Forster, relief hurler for the Dodgers, cannot recover his pitching ability because of persistent arm trouble, he should try to win a regular diamond post with his bat. In nine years Forster has gone to bat only 59 times, but he has connected for 25 hits for a fantastic career average of .424. In 1979 he went to the plate only once and received a base on balls.

* * * *

Prior to the advent of interleague play in 1995, who was the last American League hurler to hit a home run in regulation play? It was Roric Harrison, who connected for Baltimore in the second game of a twin bill with Cleveland on October 3, 1972. It came off Ray Lamb in the sixth inning of a 4–3 win over the Indians. The DH went into effect the next spring, and the biggest blow by an AL pitcher from then until 1995 was a triple by rookie Eduardo Rodriguez of Milwaukee in 1973. That was the only hit in his career of 264 games. It also was his only time at bat. Therefore the veteran relief hurler sports a lifetime 1.000 batting average and a 3.000 slugging percentage.

* * * *

In 1955 Dodger pitcher Clem Labine collected only three hits in 31 at-bats and all three hits were home runs. In fact, that's all the four-baggers he hit in his 13 years in the majors. That also was the year, 1955, when fellow Dodger hurler Sandy Koufax had his "perfect season." As a 19-year-old rookie he came to bat 12 times and fanned every time.

Of the 113 players who hit a home run in their first at-bat in the majors, 18 were pitchers. This is an amazing 16 percent, considering that the pitcher represents only 11 percent of the players on the field and is generally the weakest batter. Those breaking in with a bang in their first at-bat include:

Bill Duggleby, Philadelphia NL April 21, 1898 (grand slam)
Clise Dudley, Brooklyn NL April 27, 1929
Bill LeFebvre, Boston AL June 10, 1938
Dan Bankhead, Brooklyn NL August 26 1947
Hoyt Wilhelm, New York NL April 23, 1952
Buster Narum, Baltimore AL May 3, 1963

Donald Rose, California AL May 24, 1972
John Montefusco, San Francisco NL September 3, 1974
Jose Sosa, Houston NL July 30, 1975
Dave Eiland, San Diego NL April 10, 1992
Jim Bullinger, Chicago NL June 8, 1992
Dustin Hermanson, Montreal NL April 16, 1997
Guillermo Mota, Montreal NL June 9, 1999
Esteban Yan, Tamba Bay AL June 4, 2000
Gene Stechschulte, St. Louis NL April 17, 2001 (pinch hit)
Adam Wainwright, St. Louis NL May 24, 2006
Mark Worrell, St. Louis NL June 5, 2008
Tom Milone, Washington NL September 3, 2011

For Wilhelm, it was the only home run of his 21-year career, most of which was spent pitching in relief. It came in the fourth inning of a New York Giants game against the Boston Braves at the Polo Grounds. Giant catcher Wes Westrum had just hit a homer off Gene Conley, and the Braves brought in rookie southpaw Dick Hoover to face Wilhelm in his debut as a batter. Not to be outdone by his catcher, Hoyt dumped one into the left-field stands, not exactly a herculean feat at the Polo Grounds. He also pitched five solid innings of relief and won his first game in the majors.

Russ Van Atta didn't get any homer in his first at-bat, but he did get four singles in his first four at-bats. He also scored three runs and knocked in one in his debut for the Yankees on April 25, 1933. Oh yes, he also shut out the Senators 16–0.

* * * *

Joe Niekro has hit only one home run in the majors through the 1979 season. He connected on May 29, 1976, against Atlanta, and the opposing hurler was Phil Niekro. The blow helped Joe, pitching for Houston, to a 4–3 win over his brother.

Wes Ferrell at bat for the Boston Red Sox.

GREAT HITTING PITCHERS, 1979-2011
by Mike Cook

In the three decades since Great Hitting Pitchers was first published, a few dozen pitchers have distinguished themselves at the plate. We'll look at them in two groups: retired pitchers who played the majority of their career after 1979 and active pitchers (as of April 2012). Despite the American League's introduction of the designated hitter in 1973, and the fact that pitchers do not hit nearly as well as they once did,[1] there are some notable exceptions to the trend. In fact, when we look at rate statistics in particular, such as plate appearances per home run, we find some of baseball's best slugging hurlers among the ranks of today's active pitchers.

We'll begin by looking at retired players from recent decades. Here are the top 10 pitchers from that group, ranked by career hitting fWAR (Fangraphs WAR):

While this is a good starting point, as a career ranking it naturally favors those pitchers who enjoyed the longest careers and logged the most at-bats, even if they weren't particularly effective hitters from a rate perspective. The rate statistics below re-rank these 10 pitchers by hitting fWAR per plate appearance. Greg Maddux, who was 5th on the career list above, falls to 10th in the list below, since his relatively modest hitting totals were reached over the course of a whopping (for a pitcher) 1812 plate appearances. Also listed below are career home run totals for each pitcher, as well as his plate appearances per home run rate (lower is better).

Player	WAR (h)
Glavine, Tom	11.9
Hampton, Mike	10.8
Forsch, Bob	10.1
Rhoden, Rick	8.8
Maddux, Greg	8
Hershiser, Orel	7.7
Smoltz, John	7.5
Robinson, Don	6.9
Reuss, Jerry	6.7
Gooden, Doc	6.7

Player	WAR (h)	PA	WAR/PA	HR	PA/HR
Hampton, Mike	10.8	845	.0128	16	52.8
Rhoden, Rick	8.8	830	.0106	9	92.2
Robinson, Don	6.9	665	.0104	13	51.2
Forsch, Bob	10.1	1041	.0097	12	86.8
Hershiser, Orel	7.7	949	.0081	0	N/A
Gooden, Doc	6.7	849	.0079	8	106.1
Glavine, Tom	11.9	1645	.0072	1	1645.0
Smoltz, John	7.5	1167	.0064	5	233.4
Reuss, Jerry	6.7	1195	.0056	1	1195.0
Maddux, Greg	8	1812	.0044	5	362.4

We'll now look at some of the more interesting pitchers from the above lists, starting with the career fWAR leader of the group, Tom Glavine.

Tom Glavine

Glavine, whose major league career spanned 22 seasons (1987–2008), finds himself first on our career hitting WAR list primarily as a result of that longevity. Though he won the Silver Slugger award four times, those were all relatively modest seasons (his OPS+ for those four campaigns: 75, 48, 42, and 40). Glavine never hit .300 for a season and he only homered once in 1645 career plate appearances (among the pitchers on our retired and active leaderboards, only Orel Hershiser, with 0 home runs, hit fewer). Glavine did manage four seasons of 1.0 hitting fWAR or better. His value clearly did not come from power (career ISO power of .024), but he was an excellent sacrifice bunter and had slightly better than average plate discipline for a pitcher. Glavine totaled 216 sacrifice hits in his career and had 11 seasons with 10 or more sacrifices. His plate discipline numbers, while poor by position player standards, were better than many of the pitchers we'll be examining: he had a 6.1 BB% and 20.0 K%. For his career, Glavine was a .186/.244/.210 (AVG/OBP/SLG) hitter, but his longevity, combined with the effort he put into the fundamentals of laying down a bunt and drawing a walk, led to him topping our career hitting fWAR leaderboard.[2][3]

Mike Hampton

Mike Hampton follows Glavine on the career hitting leaderboard, but he accumulated his 10.8 fWAR in just over half as many at-bats as Glavine. Hampton ranks first when we calculate fWAR per plate appearance (.0128) and has the second-best home run rate in the group, slugging one every 52.8 plate appearances. Despite a career total of 16 home runs, Hampton didn't hit any at the beginning of his career, going homer-less in 449 plate appearances from 1994–2000. There's no doubt that his home run totals were inflated by the move to Coors Field in 2001, but Hampton was an above-average hitting pitcher in the years preceding that move as well. As an Astro in 1999, Hampton hit .311 with three doubles and three triples in 88 plate appearances, good for an .806 OPS and 104 OPS+. The following year, as a New York Met, he failed to record any extra-base hits, but did manage a .274 average. Hampton joined the Rockies in 2001, and in the final season of pre-humidor Coors Field, exploded with seven home runs. Denver's thin, dry air surely helped four of those shots, but he hit the other three on the road. The next year, 2002, was arguably Hampton's best at the plate. He slugged three home runs (with only one of them coming at Coors), but more impressively hit .344 with a career-best OPS+ of 112. Hampton won the Silver Slugger award five consecutive times from 1999-2003. In that final season he won the award based mainly on his reputation as a slugger: he hit just .183 with a 53 OPS+ that year (but did hit two more home runs). Hampton's career hitting stats certainly received a boost from his two seasons at Coors, but he should not be remembered as strictly a product of that hitting environment, seeing as it accounted for just 5 of his 16 career home runs.[4][5][6]

Bob Forsch

Bob Forsch, who wore a Cardinals' uniform for 15 of his 16 major league seasons, is third on our career hitting fWAR list at 10.1. He ranks fourth on the fWAR per plate appearance list at .0097 and hit 12 homers in his career, slugging them at a rate of one every 86.8 PAs. Forsch had three standout seasons at the plate, one each in the early, middle, and late stages of his career. In 1975, his second big league season, Forsch hit .308 (a figure that would stand up as his career best), while knocking seven extra-base hits, including three triples and a home run. That was good for an .803 OPS and 118 OPS+, which would also tie (with his 1987 campaign) for a career high. Forsch then endured a real slump at the plate, hitting no better than .181 from 1976-1979 (though 19 of his 46 hits in that span were for extra-bases, including two homers). His average bounced back in 1980 as he hit .295, continued to hit for power with five doubles and three homers, and finished with a .787 OPS and 114 OPS+. But he followed that up with his worst season in 1981, hitting just .122 with one double, for a startlingly bad -19 OPS+. Forsch was consistently mediocre for the next few years before breaking out again in 1987, at age 37, with a .298/.333/.509 line that included six doubles and two home runs. In his 16 seasons, Forsch did a nice job supplementing his value as a pitcher (30.4 career pitching fWAR) with the bat in his hands (10.1 career batting fWAR). His contributions weren't the most consistent from year to year, but in 1975, 1980, and 1987, he was a real asset to his Cardinals teams at the plate.[7][8]

Rick Rhoden

Fourth on the career hitting fWAR list (8.8), and ranking second in terms of fWAR per plate appearance (.0106), is Forsch's contemporary, Rick Rhoden. Their careers spanned the exact same 16 seasons, from 1974 to 1989. Save for a brief two-year stint with the Yankees, Rhoden pitched in the National League for the majority of his career, spending four full seasons with the Dodgers before playing the next eight in Pittsburgh. Rhoden was more consistent than Forsch, with five seasons with an OPS+ of 93 or better, including a standout year at the plate in 1980, when he hit an impressive .375 with an OPS+ of 151. Rhoden slugged three homers in 1977 and again in 1982, but totaled just nine for his career. His high ranking on the hitting fWAR leaderboards had more to do with consistently respectable batting averages, doubles power (he hit six or more in a season three times) and a low strike-out rate (at 13.7% for his career, Rhoden was harder to strikeout than many position players). Rhoden won the Silver Slugger award in three consecutive seasons, from 1984-1986. The bookends were strong campaigns (110 OPS+ in '84 and 93 OPS+ in '86), while in '85 he won largely on reputation, as he hit just .189 with an OPS+ of 24. Since he could swing the bat fairly well, Rhoden rarely bunted. He never had more than 7 sacrifices in a season, a figure Tom Glavine equaled or bested in 18 seasons. In retirement, Rhoden has continued to display an acumen for hitting the ball, only these days it's on the golf course. He has won the American Century Celebrity Golf Classic eight times, and has also made his mark among the senior professionals on the Champions Tour, with earnings of more than $250,000 and three top-10 finishes.[9] [10] [11]

Don "Caveman" Robinson

Coming in eighth on the career hitting fWAR list (6.9), but a more impressive third on the fWAR per plate appearance list (.0104) is Don "Caveman" Robinson, who was actually a teammate of Rhoden's in Pittsburgh from 1979-1986. Robinson pitched for 15 seasons and moved back and forth between the rotation and bullpen, limiting his career plate appearances to just 665. Had he been a starter, and received a starter's number of plate appearances throughout his career, Robinson's skill with the bat would be more evident. He hit 13 home runs in his career, one every 51.2 plate appearances, which is a slightly better rate than noted slugger Mike Hampton's. His best offensive seasons came early in his career in Pittsburgh, while pitching mostly as a starter. In 1980, while starting 24 games, he hit .333 with five extra-base hits and a home run in 57 plate appearances. That was good for a .789 OPS and a 116 OPS+. In 1992, he would start 30 games, batting .282 with seven XBH and two homers, equating to a .723 OPS and 98 OPS+. Robinson's power made up for some major holes in his plate discipline: he struck out more than 10 times as often as he walked in his career (168 to 16) and fell victim to the K in 25.3% of his trips to the plate. One of Robinson's more impressive feats was hitting a home run in four of five seasons from 1983-87, despite the fact that he was primarily a reliever during that period, and never had more than 35 PA in any of those years.[12][13]

Dwight "Doc" Gooden

While Dwight Gooden is only tenth on the career hitting fWAR list, he hit for decent power in relatively few plate appearances, so finds himself sixth on the fWAR/PA leaderboard. Gooden pitched in the NL for just 11 seasons, fewer than most of the pitchers we've examined, accumulating 849 plate appearances but hitting eight home runs. Gooden's strongest years as a batter actually didn't correspond to his strongest campaigns on the mound. While he was regularly among the leaders on the NL Cy Young ballot in the mid-late 1980s (winning the award in 1985), his strongest years at the plate came in the early 1990s. From 1991-93 he had four or more extra-base hits each season, winning the Silver Slugger in 1992 with five XBH including a home run. After moving over to the American League, Gooden hit his final homer as a member of the Cleveland Indians, in a 1999 interleague game. Had he enjoyed a long career exclusively in the National League, like the Braves' Glavine and Maddux, Dwight Gooden would likely be among the leaders on the career hitting fWAR list.[14][15]

ACTIVE PITCHERS

Moving on to today's active pitchers, here are the leaders in career hitting fWAR.

Again, the leaderboard contains a combination of light-hitting hurlers who've enjoyed great longevity (Livan Hernandez) as well as some true sluggers who could move to the top of this list in time, given sufficient opportunity. Note: While C.C. Sabathia is not 11th on the active list, we will include him here since his rate stats, albeit in a small sample, are quite impressive.

Now here are the rate stats fWAR per plate appearance (WAR/PA) and plate appearances per home run (PA/HR) for these ten pitchers. Notice that three veterans who rank in the top 5 in the career fWAR list (Livan Hernandez, Jason Marquis, and Randy Wolf) fall to spots 7-9 when sorted by WAR/PA.

Player	WAR (h)
Hernandez, Livan	9.4
Zambrano, Carlos	8.3
Willis, Dontrelle	6.2
Wolf, Randy	5.4
Marquis, Jason	4.9
Owings, Micah	3.8
Wainwright, Adam	3.7
Gallardo, Yovani	3.6
Peavy, Jake	3.3
Haren, Dan	2.9
Sabathia, C.C.	1.1

Player	WAR (h)	PA	WAR/PA	HR	PA/HR
Owings, Micah	3.8	217	.0175	9	24.1
Willis, Dontrelle	6.2	447	.0139	9	49.7
Gallardo, Yovani	3.6	267	.0135	9	29.7
Zambrano, Carlos	8.3	708	.0117	23	30.8
Wainwright, Adam	3.7	337	.0110	5	67.4
Sabathia, C.C.	1.1	104	.0106	3	34.7
Haren, Dan	2.9	291	.0100	2	145.5
Hernandez, Livan	9.4	1108	.0085	10	110.8
Marquis, Jason	4.9	625	.0078	5	125.0
Wolf, Randy	5.4	762	.0071	5	152.4
Peavy, Jake	3.3	482	.0068	2	241.0

Livan Hernandez

Thirty-seven-year-old Livan Hernandez leads active major league pitchers with 9.4 hitting fWAR, a figure that would put him fourth on the list of retired pitchers from recent decades, which he'll likely join soon. He's produced at a rate of .0085 WAR/PA, making him a slightly more productive hitter than some we've discussed like Glavine and Gooden, while still not being a standout contributor at the plate. Hernandez hits for a bit of power (10 HR in 1108 career PAs), but his more notable skill at the dish is simply that he puts the ball in play a lot. Both his BB% and K% are on the extreme low end for pitchers. Hernandez's walk rate is an almost non-existent 0.8% he's drawn just nine, one less than his career home run total. On the flip side, his strikeout rate of 11.6% would be quite good for a position player and is remarkably low for a hurler. It is a bit of a stretch to say that any of Hernandez's individual hitting seasons were noteworthy, but if you had to pick one, it would be 2004 in Montreal. He won the Silver Slugger award that year, hitting seven doubles and a homer, while also laying down a career-best 15 sacrifice bunts. His OPS+ was only 57 though, and he has never had a season (with more than 10 PAs) with an OPS+ of better than 91. Though Hernandez tops our career hitting fWAR leaderboard for active pitchers, he owes this to his longevity and a decent ability to put the ball in play, rather than to a high on-base or slugging percentage.[16][17]

Carlos Zambrano

Carlos Zambrano is a close second on the active pitchers leaderboard with 8.3 fWAR. At just 30 years old, he could soon pass Hernandez for the top spot, provided of course that the combustible right-hander can stay productive on the mound and in the good graces of his employers and MLB. Zambrano is a true slugging pitcher, providing much of his offensive value via the home run. He's hit 23 of them lifetime in just 708 plate appearances, a rate of one every 30.8 PAs. In 2006 Big Z had just 11 hits on the year, but a whopping six of them were round-trippers. Two years later he enjoyed his most complete offensive season, hitting .337 with nine extra-base hits, including four more homers. That was good for a .892 OPS, 122 OPS+ and 1.7 hitting fWAR. In just 85 PAs that year, he provided more value at the plate than did teammates Jim Edmonds, Kosuke Fukudome, or Reed Johnson, who all had at least 298 PAs. Zambrano has won the Silver Slugger award three times: in 2006, 2008, and again in 2009 when he pounded out five doubles and another four homers in just 72 PA. 2011, a shortened year for Zambrano due to his suspension (and threatened retirement), still included impressive contributions at the plate: a .313 AVG with four XBH (two doubles, two homers) in just 48 PAs. If there's a downside to Zambrano's hitting, it's his plate discipline: the free-swinger has managed a walk rate almost as low as Hernandez's (1.4%) while whiffing in nearly one third of his trips to the plate (32.8%). For the 2012 season, Zambrano leaves baseball's second-oldest ballpark to play his home games at its newest venue, Marlins Park. Time will tell if the changes of scenery and manager suit him well.[18] [19] [20]

Dontrelle Willis

Few would guess that Dontrelle Willis ranks third on our list of active pitchers by hitting fWAR. Though he is also 30 years old, Willis has 261 fewer plate appearances than Zambrano. He won the NL Rookie of the Year as a 21-year-old with the Marlins in 2003, but since leaving their organization after the 2007 season, he's made no more than 13 starts in a season, playing for three different clubs in that time. Despite his inconsistencies on the mound, Willis has excelled at the plate both in his early days as a Marlin and last year with the Reds. Dontrelle's finest offensive season was 2007, when he hit .286 with an .856 OPS, thanks to seven extra-base hits (two doubles, three triples, and two homers) in just 80 plate appearances. In most years those numbers would be Silver Slugger-worthy, but Willis had the misfortune of being compared to Micah Owings, whose 2007 ranks as one of the greatest hitting seasons by a pitcher of all time (more on him later). After spending a couple of seasons in the American League with Detroit, Willis resumed his sweet-swinging ways without missing a beat when he returned to the NL in 2011. Despite receiving only 34 plate appearances last year, he made the most of them, crushing five extra-base hits, including a triple and a homer, while hitting .387 and even laying down three sacrifice bunts. Dontrelle Willis is one of the most complete hitting pitchers of our era: his average (.244) and plate discipline (4.9 BB%, 15.4 K%) are both excellent by pitchers' standards, and his combination of strength and speed have produced many extra-base hits (13 doubles, six triples, and nine home runs for his career). Ultimately, Willis's ability to rank even higher on this list will depend on his returning to form on the mound. If he can do that though, there's no reason to think that one of today's most productive hitting pitchers can't post some lofty career hitting totals.[21] [22]

Micah Owings

In Micah Owings we have a hitter of such impact that he might more aptly be included in the book "Great Pitching Hitters" than in our collection of the "Great Hitting Pitchers." Owings, 29 years old, has just 217 career plate appearances, but his production in those has been above replacement level by position player standards, never mind a pitcher's. Take the WAR per plate appearance metric for example. Owings ranks first among the pitchers on our retired and active lists by a wide margin, coming in at .0175 WAR/PA, while the next best is Willis at .0139. Back in college, scouts saw Owings put up team-leading numbers both at the plate and on the mound. As a junior at Tulane in 2005, he led the Green

Wave in home runs (18) and in pitching strikeouts (131). He started 61 games in the field (splitting his time between 1B, DH, and LF) while also starting 18 games on the mound. In his age-24 rookie season in the bigs (2007), Owings exploded onto the scene. In just 64 PAs he hit .333 with a 1.033 OPS and a 152 OPS+, knocking 12 extra-base hits including four home runs. He deservedly took home the Silver Slugger award, and it would come as no surprise to see him win several more. His next best season came in 2009 when he hit for an .818 OPS and 110 OPS+, hitting for excellent power again with eight XBH (including three home runs) in just 58 PAs. For his career, Owings has already accumulated 3.8 hitting fWAR in only about a third of a position player's yearly plate appearances (217). He's hit a home run once every 24.1 PAs, slugged .507, and posted a career OPS+ of 108, better than league-average. Though he strikes out a lot (32.3 K%), Owings is in every other respect a very solid hitter, standing head and shoulders above the other slugging pitchers on this list. As with Willis, if he can pitch effectively enough to stick in the big leagues and remains in the National League (he signed with San Diego for the 2012 season), there's no telling what kind of career hitting totals Owings can amass. [23] [24] [25] [26]

Yovani Gallardo

Of the active pitchers we've discussed so far, Yovani Gallardo has been arguably the most successful on the mound, while also helping his cause quite often at the plate. After his age-25 season, he's totaled 13.4 fWAR pitching and another 3.6 fWAR hitting. In 2007, his rookie year, he knocked five extra-base hits (three doubles and two homers) in just 42 plate appearances. As we've noted, 2007 was a big year for hitting pitchers in the National League, with Dontrelle Willis and Micah Owings also enjoying career years. In 2010 Gallardo posted even stronger totals, hitting for an .837 OPS and 122 OPS+ thanks to eight extra-base hits (four doubles and four homers) in 72 plate appearances. That year he did win the Silver Slugger award, after Carlos Zambrano had taken the honor in three of the previous four years. Gallardo's most memorable single-game performance came in early 2009, when he shut down the visiting Pirates on the hill and provided all the offense his team would need at the plate. On April 29, he tossed eight innings of scoreless two-hit ball, striking out 11, while also hitting a solo home run to account for the only scoring in the Brewers' 1–0 victory. Of the pitchers on our list, Gallardo's PA/HR rate of 29.7 (9 HR in 267 career PAs) ranks second only to Micah Owings, but as an elite starting pitcher, Gallardo should have the opportunity to rack up many more at-bats in the years ahead. Given his combination of age, pitching skill, and prowess at the plate, it would come as no surprise to see Gallardo at the top of our hitting pitchers leaderboard when his career is done.[27] [28]

C.C. Sabathia

C.C. Sabathia has spent the vast majority of his career in the American League (338 of his 355 starts have come with the Indians and Yankees) and has accumulated just 1.1 hitting fWAR. He warrants inclusion here though for the impressive rate stats he's generated in the small sample of his 104 plate appearances. The hefty lefty has mashed three home runs in his career, for a PA/HR rate of 34.7, ranking behind only Owings, Gallardo, and Zambrano among active pitchers, and better than all of the pitchers on our retired leaderboard. Sabathia provided some offensive spark to the Brewers following his trade to Milwaukee in mid-2007, where he joined fellow slugging pitcher Yovani Gallardo in the rotation. As a Brewer Sabathia hit .229 in 50 plate appearances, but that included a home run, two doubles, and six RBIs. Having signed an extension with the Yankees through 2017, it's unlikely that Sabathia will get too many more chances at the plate. When he does get those at-bats in interleague play, or in future World Series, Sabathia's a better bet than most AL hurlers to make an impact with the bat.[29] [30]

* * * *

While pitcher hitting has declined over the decades, and there are those who would prefer to see the designated hitter adopted universally across baseball, the players discussed here are proof that not all pitchers are one dimensional. In some cases their contributions were marginal, but a long career of 1,000 plate appearances or more has lifted them to the top of our career leaderboards. Others are better hitters on a rate basis, but their plate contributions have been limited by their inconsistent pitching or by playing in the American League. Rare are those who excel both at the plate and on the mound, who have posted excellent hitting rate stats while also enjoying a long pitching career. Of the retired group, Mike Hampton best fits that description, and among the active set, Yovani Gallardo has the chance to put up similar or better numbers.

Each pitcher's story is unique. Whether they're included here for hitting six home runs in a season like Carlos Zambrano, or for laying down 216 sacrifice bunts in a career like Tom Glavine, all belong in the fraternity of the Great Hitting Pitchers.

ENDNOTES

1. A 2007 study by David Gassko of The Hardball Times compared the weighted on-base average (wOBA) for pitchers and position players from 1871 to 2005. The ratio of pitchers' wOBA to position players' wOBA has steadily declined over the years, from the range of 0.95-1.00 in the 1870s and '80s to about 0.50 from 1990 onward. Most of that decline happened prior to the AL's introduction of the DH in 1973; at that time the ratio of pitcher to position player wOBA was already in the range of 0.55. http://www.hardballtimes.com/main/article/hitting-pitchers/
2. http://www.baseball-reference.com/players/g/glavito02-bat.shtml
3. http://www.fangraphs.com/statss.aspx?playerid=90&position=PB
4. http://www.baseball-reference.com/players/h/hamptmi01-bat.shtml
5. http://www.fangraphs.com/statss.aspx?playerid=430&position=PB
6. http://www.fangraphs.com/blogs/index.php/hamptons-hitting/
7. http://www.fangraphs.com/statss.aspx?playerid=1004233&position=PB
8. http://www.baseball-reference.com/players/f/forscbo01-bat.shtml
9. http://www.baseball-reference.com/players/r/rhoderi01-bat.shtml
10. http://www.fangraphs.com/statss.aspx?playerid=1010887&position=PB
11 http://en.wikipedia.org/wiki/Rick_Rhoden#Life_after_baseball:_a_second_career_in_golf
12. http://www.fangraphs.com/statss.aspx?playerid=1011061&position=PB
13. http://www.baseball-reference.com/players/r/robindo01-bat.shtml
14. http://www.fangraphs.com/statss.aspx?playerid=1004852&position=PB
15. http://www.baseball-reference.com/players/g/goodedw01-bat.shtml
16. http://www.baseball-reference.com/players/h/hernali01-bat.shtml
17. http://www.fangraphs.com/statss.aspx?playerid=1116&position=PB
18. http://www.baseball-reference.com/players/z/zambrca01-bat.shtml
19. http://www.fangraphs.com/statss.aspx?playerid=305&position=PB
20. http://www.fangraphs.com/leaders.aspx?pos=all&stats=bat&lg=all&qual=0&type=8&season=2008&month=0&season1=2008&ind=0&team=17&rost=0
21. http://www.baseball-reference.com/players/w/willido03-bat.shtml
22. http://www.fangraphs.com/statss.aspx?playerid=1703&position=PB
23. http://www.baseball-reference.com/players/o/owingmi01-bat.shtml
24. http://www.fangraphs.com/statss.aspx?playerid=4253&position=PB

25. http://www.fangraphs.com/fantasy/index.php/owings-aims-for-pitching-accolades/
26. http://www.tulanegreenwave.com/sports/m-basebl/mtt/owings_micah00.html
27. http://www.fangraphs.com/statss.aspx?playerid=8173&position=PB
28. http://www.baseball-reference.com/players/g/gallayo01-bat.shtml
29. http://www.baseball-reference.com/players/s/sabatc.01-bat.shtml
30. http://www.fangraphs.com/statss.aspx?playerid=404&position=PB.

THE SABR DIGITAL LIBRARY

The Society for American Baseball Research, the top baseball research organization in the world, disseminates some of the best in baseball history, analysis, and biography through our publishing programs. The SABR Digital Library focuses on a tandem program of paperback and ebook publication, making material widely available for sale on both digital devices and as traditional books.

SABR members may purchase the printed books at a drastically reduced price, and download the ebook editions free upon first release and then at a discount in the future. Among the recent releases in The SABR Digital Library you will find:

CAN HE PLAY? A LOOK AT BASEBALL SCOUTS AND THEIR PROFESSION

CAN HE PLAY? touches on more than a century of scouts and scouting with a focus on the men (and the occasional woman) who have taken on the task of scouring the world for the best ballplayers available. Including close to 100 photos, over 35 biographies, and multiple essays and interviews, and involving the contributions of 26 SABR members and the SABR Scouts Committee, CAN HE PLAY? is the definitive source on scouts and scouting.
Paperback: $19.95 non-members, $9.95 SABR Members
Ebook: $9.99 non-members, free to SABR Members until February 29, 2012

RUN, RABBIT, RUN

The Hiliarious and Mostly True Stories of Rabbit Maranville
Paperback: $9.95 non-members, $5.00 members
Ebooks; $5.99 non-members, free to SABR Members unti
March 1, 2012
Rabbit's anecdotes of his 38 years in organized
baseball, plus photos, an intro by Harold
Seymour, and a biographical essay by Bob
Carroll.

Made in the USA
Columbia, SC
03 November 2021